KAA

BOOM

How to Engage the 50-Plus Worker and Beat the Workforce Crisis

Barb Jaworski

Barbara Jaworski

Workplace Institute
Engagement Model for 50-Plus Workers™

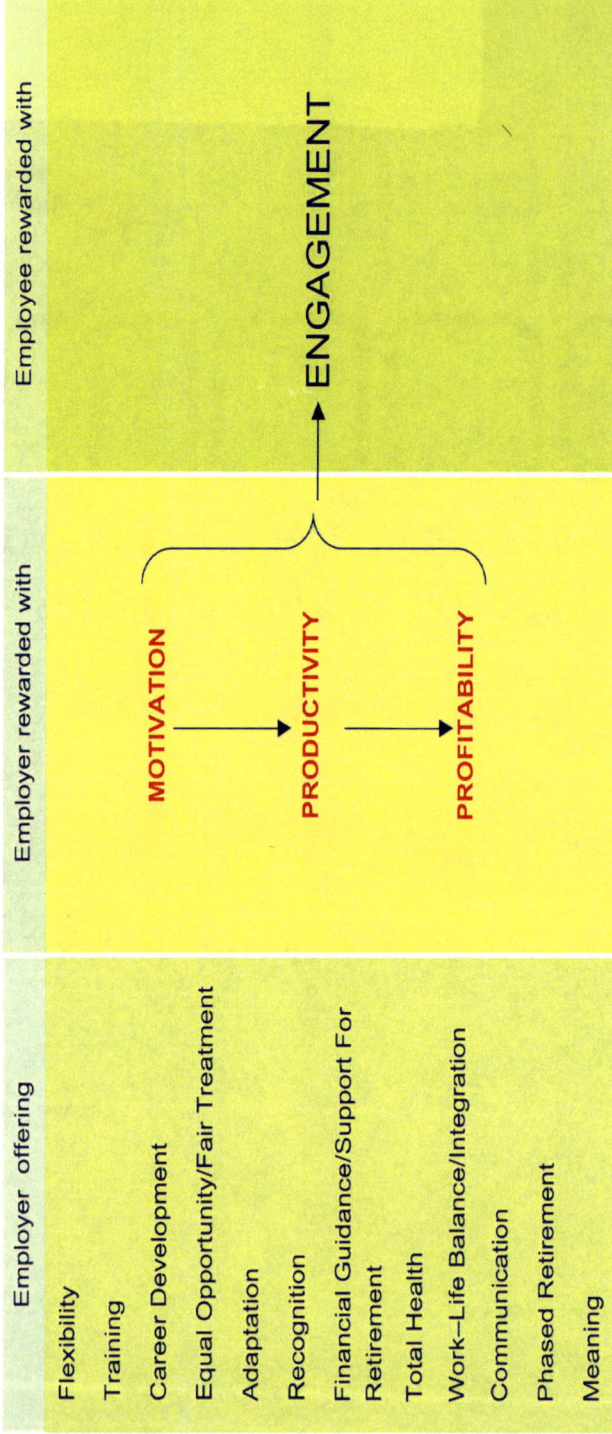

Employer offering

- Flexibility
- Training
- Career Development
- Equal Opportunity/Fair Treatment
- Adaptation
- Recognition
- Financial Guidance/Support For Retirement
- Total Health
- Work–Life Balance/Integration
- Communication
- Phased Retirement
- Meaning

Employer rewarded with

MOTIVATION → PRODUCTIVITY → PROFITABILITY

Employee rewarded with

ENGAGEMENT

WORKPLACE
INSTITUTE

I would like to dedicate this to my family, Gareth, Alexandra and Katherine, for their unfailing support and encouragement throughout the writing of this book.

The Workplace Institute™ gratefully acknowledges the ongoing creative leadership of the *Best Employers Award for 50 Plus Canadians™* winners who continue to lead the way in harnessing the skills of all workers. Their gracious permission to publish their strategies and tactics so that others can learn from their experience is greatly appreciated. In particular I would like to thank Ben Lenton, Jane Gibbens, Claude Graziadei, Terry Daly, Jean Fader, Cathy Lim, Trevor Skillen, Dr. Leroy Stone, Gary Fry, Ruth Hart, Beth Kingzett, Jim Brady, Louise Leith, Carrie Solmundson, Eve Simpson, Angie Goldsmith, Elizabeth Lincoln, Sharon Galloway, Joy Haverston and Britt Wilson. A special thanks to Andrina Buffong, my colleague at Mitre Corporation, who over the years has been an invaluable sounding board, Gay Stinson, HRSDC, whose critical insights and feedback kept me focused, and Moira Potter, for her contribution to the book.
Editor: Ann MacNaughton
Cover concept/design: Soloteam.ca

Written by	Barbara Jaworski	bjaworski@workplaceinstitute.org
	Workplace Institute™	2239 Bloor St. W Suite 4
		Toronto, ON
		Canada M6S 1N7
		Phone 416–704–3517
		Fax 416–762–7265
		www.workplaceinstitute.org

ISBN 1-4251-1624-8   First Edition

Note for Librarians: A cataloguing record for this book is available from Library and Archives Canada at www.collectionscanada.ca/amicus/index-e.html
ISBN 1-4251-1624-8

Printed in Victoria, BC, Canada. Printed on paper with minimum 30% recycled fibre.
Trafford's print shop runs on "green energy" from solar, wind and other environmentally-friendly power sources.

Trafford
PUBLISHING
Offices in Canada, USA, Ireland and UK

Book sales for North America and international:
Trafford Publishing, 6E–2333 Government St., Victoria, BC V8T 4P4 CANADA
phone 250 383 6864 (toll-free 1 888 232 4444) fax 250 383 6804; email to orders@trafford.com
Book sales in Europe:
Trafford Publishing (UK) Limited, 9 Park End Street, 2nd Floor
Oxford, UK OX1 1HH UNITED KINGDOM
phone +44 (0)1865 722 113 (local rate 0845 230 9601) facsimile +44 (0)1865 722 868; info.uk@trafford.com **Order online at:** trafford.com/07-0033

10 9 8 7 6 5 4 3

Barbara Jaworski

Barbara Jaworski, founder of the Workplace
Institute, is Canada's leading expert on the
50-plus workforce. Highly regarded as a human resources consultant,
she specializes in the fields of employee engagement, organizational
branding, work-life, health and productivity. Over the years she has
developed innovative programs and services for more than 2100
organizations in Canada and globally.

She has developed the annual *Best Employers Award for 50 Plus
Canadians*™, now going into its fourth year, as well as the annual
Summit on the Mature Workforce. These initiatives are coordinated
through the Workplace Institute. Jaworski has also designed and
implemented Work Life Solutions—a wide range of programs that
comprise one of the most comprehensive and innovative work-life
and wellness and disease management services in the industry. She
helps organizations unleash the productivity of 50-plus workers
through a number of new and innovative strategies derived from her
own and others' latest research. Jaworski currently chairs the U.S.-
based annual Alliance of Work-Life Progress Work-Life Innovation
Excellence Awards.

She regularly speaks at conferences throughout North America.
A frequent contributor to health and benefits publications and
journals, she is also consulted by the media and has been quoted
extensively in radio, TV and newspapers, including *The Globe
and Mail*.

She lives in Toronto with her husband of 19 years and two
teenaged daughters.

Contents

1

Why Care About the 50-Plus Worker?

The Home Depot secret

Home Depot is the world's largest home improvement retailer. Associated Press reported its 2006 revenue at $79.5 billion. It caters to do-it-yourselfers as well as professional builders in seven Canadian provinces, 49 U.S. states, Puerto Rico and Mexico. Consumers obviously love Home Depot—in Canada alone the company opens 20 new stores a year.

What is the secret of its success? Home Depot is doing a lot of things right, but one key element is superb customer service. Feedback has shown that consumers with a do-it-yourself puzzle choose Home Depot as their first stop because they know they will find a sales associate who sincerely wants to help. Home Depot associates come from the construction or design professions, the trades, or are committed do-it-yourselfers themselves. They offer customers in-depth product knowledge, personal experience of home improvement and, most importantly, people skills.

But there's something else different about Home Depot employees: their age. It's no accident that they are decidedly older than the usual sales personnel found in other retail outlets. Several years ago, Home Depot realized that their 50-plus workers were less likely to leave, less likely to be absent, could work weekend, early-morning and late-day shifts, and often preferred part-time work. Fifty-plus staff members obviously enjoyed their jobs and appreciated the highly structured training program for each department with twice-yearly performance evaluations. Customers liked relating to staff in their own age bracket—and since homeowners are generally older, it made good business sense for Home Depot to reflect that demographic in its retail staff.

The 50-plus advantage

Home Depot is only one outstanding winner of a *Best Employers Award for 50 Plus Canadians*™. The 16 winners to date are a diverse group from both the public and private sector—and all are capitalizing on the experience, stability, knowledge and loyalty older workers bring to the job. These nimble organizations recognize how the skills, talents and experience of their 50-plus workforce can help their businesses excel.

Many other companies are following their lead and are now beginning to target 50-plus workers, realizing the enormous advantages this demographic offers employers.

This book reveals the strategies and initiatives *Best Employers Award for 50 Plus Canadians*™ winners have created to capitalize on the mature workforce and forestall the coming talent crunch—strategies and initiatives your organization can tailor to meet its own unique needs.

Organizations and the 50-plus worker: definitions

An organization is a private business, corporation, provincial, federal, municipal, crown corporation, not-for-profit or nonprofit entity that is organized to produce a product or service for others.

The 50-plus demographic is often called the "mature" workforce, but the terms "50-plus", "mature" and "older" are used interchangeably throughout this book. To most, 50 is the time when we approach our prime working years, with the wisdom and experience that makes us valuable to any organization. Ironically, it's at 50 that most people begin finding it very difficult to get new employment. It's around that age that many organizations begin wanting to lay employees off or ease them into "early retirement" in order to get "cheaper, fresher and more enthusiastic" workers.

Why 50-plus workers are great for organizations

Fifty-plus workers:
- are engaged (contrary to popular belief)
- are loyal
- are reliable and take less time off work
- understand the corporate culture
- need less supervision
- boost profits and service delivery
- cost an employer less (because they are less likely to leave for the next new experience).

The Society for Human Resource Management (SHRM) conducted a survey in which half the respondents felt that younger workers lack professionalism, business knowledge and communication, writing and analytical skills.[1] Pretty harsh words, but it sounds as

---

1.   SHRM/NOWCC/CED, *Older Worker Survey*, SHRM Research, 2003.

if there are a lot of frustrated employers who aren't finding what they need when they put out their "Help Wanted" signs. Maybe that's because they're looking in all the wrong places. Recruiters constantly complain that their organization clients have unrealistic expectations, asking for highly skilled people with a broad range of experiences who are about 35 years old. It just does not compute!

The aging workforce crisis

Employers today face a very real and dangerous aging workforce crisis. To put it bluntly, organizations must learn to maximize the potential of mature workers, or perish. Already, hundreds of businesses are closing because of workforce shortages, haemorrhaging productivity and profitability as millions of baby boomers—fully one third of the workforce—retire, leaving talent shortages in their wake. Canada's healthcare, construction, energy, and oil and mining sectors are already feeling the effects of too many departing older workers and too few younger, skilled replacements.

Organizations need to start making changes to their workforce practices today.

The silver lining

Successful organizations must develop a structured approach tailored specifically to attract, challenge and retain the 50-plus worker. Mature workers will become an ever-more valuable resource as organizations struggle to compete for reliable, knowledgeable and skilled workers. Workforce demographics will make that competition increasingly ferocious.

But organizations aren't very good yet at understanding how to get the best from the 50-plus worker. Erroneous myths about older workers are often accepted at face value. Employer red flags and excuses designed to discourage employment of this demographic—

such as the potential increase in benefit costs—simply don't stand up to scrutiny and need to be removed.

Despair not. A few forward-looking organizations have seized the many opportunities that an aging workforce offers and have shown different ways to unleash the potential of this undervalued group. This guide contains numerous examples of how businesses and governments have turned a black cloud into one with a truly silver lining.

Best practices for the 50-plus workforce

This guide is intended for senior leaders, talent managers, recruiters, operational managers and Human Resources professionals charged with changing organizational practices and policies in order to meet the challenges of an aging workforce and skills shortages. Designing best practices for a mature workforce is a new field, one that will receive a lot of attention in the coming years. There is a lot to learn if organizations are going to attract and retain the workers they need now and in the future.

North America has an exploding older population and outdated legislation regarding retirement and pensions. North American organizations need to answer some tough questions—the answers to which will make the difference between surviving or stumbling in the years to come. Questions like these: Will we continue to benignly discriminate against older, experienced workers? Will we abolish mandatory retirement altogether, as has already been done in many jurisdictions? Can we find ways to get around skills shortages? Can our business deal with large pension deficits? Can different options be found for retirees who want to continue working or will they have to go to our competitors?

It's a time of discomfort in the workplace for employees and employers alike thanks to outdated policies and practices. If organizations continue to discriminate again their experienced workers, those workers will walk or run to competing firms at the first opportunity. Those companies who understand the demographics and who are creating innovative programs and policies to attract, retain and motivate older workers will reap the rewards. Those who do not will lose the war for talent as the best and brightest, young and old, go elsewhere.

That war has already begun.

CHAPTER 2

Trends Shaping Workforce Strategy and the Coming Crisis

So you don't think you have a problem?

All provinces except P.E.I. and Quebec are now experiencing skill shortages, with Alberta and British Columbia currently experiencing the most acute scarcity. And this situation will only worsen. By 2016, Statistics Canada predicts that the demand for workers will outpace supply while the Conference Board predicts the crisis will begin by 2010.

Organizations are now finding that they can't attract employees of the calibre they want.

Companies like Home Depot are ramping up across Canada and the continent looking for sales help at time when the retail industry overall can't find enough workers. There is an alarming, and growing, shortage of doctors, nurses and other health professionals across the country. In booming Alberta, builders can't keep up with the exploding population's demand for housing due to a severe shortage of skilled tradespeople. In Quebec, biotech industries are recruiting from France. The defence and aerospace industries in Halifax can't find tradespeople either and are developing mentoring programs for high school girls in the hope that one day, those girls will consider entering their industries.

Another factor contributing to the workforce scarcity problem is short-sighted retirement policies. Government and company pension rules do not currently motivate people to continue working past the age of 65 if they choose to do so. Many companies would gladly hire back retired workers, but pension clawbacks make returning to the workforce financially impractical for many.

Workers are still mandated to retire at 65 in Alberta, British Columbia, Nova Scotia, New Brunswick, Newfoundland and P.E.I. For Alberta and British Columbia in particular, any increase in the retirement age would help address their current skills shortages.

Allowing skilled workers into Canada through work visas or immigration could alleviate the shortage in some sectors. Unfortunately, many of the credentialing rules that allow newcomers to practice in their area of expertise are outdated. Many skilled people are simply unable to practice their professions without lengthy re-accreditations; some are never able to overcome all the barriers that the regulatory bodies pose or the caps that are maintained. To top it off, each provincial licensing body has different standards and little incentive to fast-track capable immigrants.

This slowdown in labour force growth will continue to challenge businesses and put workers in the driver seat.

How did we get here? What forces have led to the workforce shortage?

Workforce Generations	
VETERANS:	born 1945 or earlier
BABY BOOMERS:	born 1946–1966
GEN X:	born 1967–1979
GEN Y:	born 1980 and after

Trend one: the aging workforce

Canada's working population is aging. There are now more people over the age of 60 than under the age of five, and that ratio is not expected to change any time soon. The only cohort expected to expand in the North American labour force in the next 45 years is the 55-plus group and it will start with a "boom" as the large number of early baby boomers enter this category. The 55–64 workforce will have net increases of 60–70% through 2010, with the majority of the increase occurring by 2025.[2]

Since 1994, there has been a concerted effort to get rid of older workers. Employees have been leaving the workforce in their 50s, some with pensions and early retirement packages to encourage them to go. This worked to lower the average age of employees for a while but that trend is changing, as employers in all industries notice that the average age of their workforce is rising due to the sheer numbers of boomers. Continuing to retire people early would mean too many experienced people leaving at once.

Men on average are retiring at 62, but their exit from the workforce has slowed due to poor performance of pension and investment instruments, resulting in lower-than-expected retirement incomes. Still, the overall participation rate of men in the workplace is decreasing rapidly. In 1947, 47.5% of men

2.   Calculation from *Population Projections for Canada, Provinces and Territories 2000–2026*, Statistics Canada, Catalogue No. 91–520 (2003).

over the age of 65 continued to work and in 1953, 86.5% of men between the ages of 55–64 were in the workforce. In 2004, only 66% of men aged 55 and 64 remained in the labour force with just 11.8% of those over 65 working. This is a stunning retreat from the workforce for men.

Women, on the other hand, increasingly work later in life. In 1954 only 12.9% of women aged 55–64 were in the labour force, compared to 47.7% in 2004. The labour force participation rates of women over 65 have never exceeded the rate of 6.3% set in 1964. Women's median retirement age also dropped from 64.8 in 1976 to 60.8 in 2004.[3]

According to some studies, approximately 50% of the working population expect to work beyond the age of 65. Financial necessity is clearly one of the most important reasons. But from employee surveys, we learn that many of these individuals not only need, but *want* to continue to work for a variety of positive reasons. They want to feel they are contributing to society and that they are both valued and valuable. They want the social networks that the workplace may provide. These important insights can provide an opportunity for employers astute enough to take advantage of them.[4]

Another Statistics Canada study in 2004 (looking at the 2002 General Social Survey data with those 45–59) cited that 18.4% of Canadians 45–59 years old did not plan on retiring at all. These are two extremes reflecting a reality that probably sits somewhere in between, depending on what other forces—such as debt load, interesting work, health, social supports and family—are at play.[5]

3. Leroy Stone, *New Frontiers of Research on Retirement*, Statistics Canada, Catalogue No. 75–511–XPE (2006), 143–146.

4. BMO Ipsos Reid, *Retirement Trends Study* (2006).

5. G. Schellenberg, *The Retirement Plans and Expectations of Non-Retired Canadians Aged 45 to 50*, Business and Labour Market Analysis Division, Statistics Canada, Catalogue No. 11F0010MIF2004223, Ottawa (2004).

Trend two: longer lifespan

In 2006 the first group of baby boomers reached the age of 60. Many early boomers find it hard to identify themselves as "older" or "aging" or even "mature." After all, isn't 60 the new 40? And don't call them seniors. Seniors are their parents! Many boomers still recall the 60s mantra not to trust anyone over the age of 30.

In the U.S., those turning 50 are often shocked to find an application to join the American Association of Retired Persons (AARP) arriving in their mail. Retired? Them? It's just something to which those hitting 50 cannot relate. In fact, the 50–75 demographic is more active than any previous generation has been.

Boomers as a group are less likely to "act their age" and refuse to accept expectations of how they should behave. They continue to pursue the activities of their youth and to seek out new experiences.

Veterans (those born between 1922 and 1945) are changing too. A study by the National Council on Aging (NCOA) in the U.S., *Myths and Realities of Aging 2000,* examined the American attitude toward aging. The good news is that they found those older than 18 want to live to 90. Forty-four per cent of those older than 65 said their present age was the best time of their lives. This is a dramatic shift in attitude from the original NCOA survey in 1975, in which only 32% felt that the years past 65 were the best of their lives. Veterans' lives are more interesting and fulfilling and they are going full steam ahead.

Veterans are also living longer. From 1990 to 2001 there was a dramatic 40% increase in the number of "oldest old" in our population, with continued substantial growth expected in this cohort.[6] This means that we will have longer working lives if we choose to, longer than we had ever dreamed.

---

6. *Caring for an aging population,* 2001 Census of Population, Statistics Canada, Catalogue No. 89–582–XIE (2001).

Trend three: chronic health concerns at a younger age

Though relatively healthy, boomers may turn out to be less healthy than their parents. There are rumblings in the literature and from the workplace that more people than ever are suffering from the silent killer of metabolic disorders, a grouping of symptoms that include high blood pressure, high cholesterol, being overweight and having a high body mass index (BMI). Unfortunately for those suffering from these silent killers, quality of life will be diminished for 10 to 20 years before the final *coup de grace* of a fatal stroke or heart attack. Workplace health data also shows that employees in their 30s are beginning to show signs of chronic disease, a worrying indication of the deteriorating health of the youngest workers.

As the workforce continues to age, the rate of chronic health conditions, such as diabetes, cancer and cardiovascular disease, increase. For the last decade, drug usage for high blood pressure, cholesterol and diabetes has skyrocketed. Does this mean chronic diseases are inevitable with age, or that people have health risks that will eventually have a negative affect on their future productivity and quality of life?

In fact, evidence shows that lifestyle choices, not age, are to blame. Individuals who do not modify their behaviour to include healthy eating, regular exercise, weight control, moderate alcohol consumption, and abstention from smoking will find themselves in possession of an increasingly unhealthy body. Workers who take fewer risks with their health will continue to be valuable contributors to an organization and fit enough to work well past the age of 65.

The cost of poor lifestyle choices for benefit and health plans is such that some organizations in the U.S. are beginning to disqualify applications from or dismiss smokers because of the known cost implications to their health plans. This is currently legal in the following states: Texas, Arkansas, Idaho, Washington, Tennessee, Arizona, Kansas and the City of Omaha. We know that health risks can be quantified at $2000 per risk per person in Canada, while in the U.S. the cost doubles to $4000.

Chronic disease will be the future wildcard in many organizations, especially as more workers take advantage of being able to stay after the age of 65.

Trend four: more women in the workforce

Women constitute a growing portion of the workforce. Seventy-six percent of women 45–54 have a full—or part-time job and they are an increasing segment of the older workforce.[7] This will mean a significant pool of potential employees in the coming war for talent.

Past studies hypothesized that women would leave the workforce in large numbers to look after aging parents. That is simply not happening. Women are definitely the main caregivers, but there is a reluctance to leave the workforce and make caregiving a full-time job. It is unclear if this is because they cannot afford to leave, or whether the choice is made for other reasons.

In the 1960s, young women began to delay childbirth, or not have children at all. Instead they focused on forging careers or pursuing a post-secondary education. This trend of delaying childbirth until one's 30s or even 40s continues in the present as younger women follow the trails blazed by their mothers and establish successful careers. Even childbirth does not cause most women to leave today's workforce. Whether for career or financial motives, many choose to raise a family and pursue a career simultaneously.

Even after paying for their children's post-secondary education, more and more women are staying in the workforce longer in order not to lose their source of independent income, benefits and pension.

---

7.   Leroy Stone and Lynn MacDonald, *New Frontiers of Research on Retirement*, Statistics Canada, Catalogue No. 75–511–XPE (2006), 143–146.

Trend five: a more diverse workforce

There are now four distinct generations that make up our workforce, each with its own values, expectations, working and communications styles. There are the "veterans," those born in1945 or earlier who, if still in the workforce, are usually in more senior positions. Following them is the huge post-WWII "baby boomer" generation of 40– to 60-year-olds who comprise one-third of the workforce. Scaling the corporate ladder behind the boomers is the small "Gen X" demographic born between 1967 and 1979. Last but by no means least is the larger "Generation Y"—the children of the baby boomers—who are just now beginning to enter the workplace. This four-generation range is prevalent in most developed countries, especially North America, Western Europe, Australia and Japan.

Motivating and inspiring each group requires the skills of an orchestra conductor. The good news is that there is a lot of information available about what younger groups need and want. Managers now need to incorporate this information into their growing understanding of the 50-plus workforce.

In addition to age diversity, the North American workforce is becoming more ethnically diverse as a rising tide of immigrants adds much-needed skills to our talent-scarce workforce. Managers also need to understand and learn how to motivate ethnically diverse groups.

Trend six: the declining birth rate

Much has been written about the declining birthrate in the developed world. Since the 1970s, the Canadian birthrate has been below the replacement level of 2.1.[8] In the early 1960s women were having four children on average. By 1996[9] that figure was

---

8. Statistics Canada, *The Daily*, March 13, 2001.

9. Statistics Canada, *The Daily*, March 13, 2001.

1.62. In 2003, births were up for the first time in a decade and a baby "boomlet" was declared when the number of births rose to 1.51, up from a record low of 1.49 set in 2000.[10] The birthrate is now expected to fall even further.

There is limited government support for families in North America. With the lowest birthrate in the country, the Quebec government is developing some of the most innovative solutions in the Western world, such as $5-a-day daycare to alleviate one of the most costly issues for families.[11] This incentive has resulted in more women entering the Quebec workforce whereas in Alberta, with its limited support of daycare, more and more women are withdrawing from the labour pool.

Trend seven: changing family structure and work-life imbalance

Families in the early 21st century bear little resemblance to those of 50, or even 20, years ago. The "traditional" nuclear family of mom, dad and 2.5 kids is no longer the norm. High divorce rates have made blended families common, with mom and her two kids from her first marriage marrying dad with his three kids from his previous two marriages. High divorce rates have also meant more people shouldering the burdens of parenthood alone. The fact that both men and women are delaying having children until their 30s and 40s has resulted in what is called the "sandwich generation"—individuals simultaneously tending to the needs of both young children and elderly parents. Our increasingly diverse population includes many from cultures where parents, children and their children occupy the same residence.

Unlike the "traditional" family of previous generations, where one parent (the father) was the primary breadwinner and the

---

10.   "Ontario Leading the Baby Boomlet," Toronto Star, August 12, 2003, 22.

11.   "Population Key to Ontario's Health," Globe and Mail, January 9, 2004.

other (the mother) stayed at home tending to the needs of the family, in today's family both parents juggle job and family needs. In today's wired world many are expected to work from home during the evenings and weekends to keep on top of mounting job demands. If this isn't enough of a strain on family life, add the high cost of living downtown, which is forcing more of us to commute from the ever-expanding suburbs. It's not unusual for employees to travel one or two hours to their place of work as well as work more shiftwork.

Changing family structures, increased work demands, technology and commuting mean people simply do not have enough time to devote to their family responsibilities and social pursuits. We're losing the battle for work-life balance.

But increasingly, people are fighting back. The demand for better work-life balance will become more of an issue for mature workers who have worked those long hours, established their careers and are financially stable, and who now want to concentrate their energies on their personal lives. Younger workers do not want to make the same mistakes as their parents. They want to spend time with their children, spouse and friends. They want to travel. They want to devote time to volunteer activities.

Understanding the growing importance of work-life balance is key for organizations who want to attract—and retain—skilled, talented employees of any age.

Trend eight: lengthier retirement

Retirement is a relatively new social construct. In the U.S. it was implemented at the height of the Depression to help create jobs for younger workers. Before then, people worked until they were physically incapable. Life expectancy in the first decades of the 1900s was less than 65. Now it's 83 for women and 81 for men.

When the U.S. established its pension system in 1935, it was meant to support an employee for one to two years, not the 20–30 year retirement range it is now expected to sustain. According to

Statistics Canada men retire at the average age of 61.8, while women retire at the median age of 60.8 (in 2004).[12] In Europe, only 4% of adults work to 65.

Both the public and private systems that support those in their old age were never meant to do so for so long. These supports consist of Social Security and health care in the U.S., and the Canada Pension Plan, Old Age Security and the Drug Benefit Plan in Canada (health care is paid for all Canadians). The systems in Canada are self-sustaining through adjustments made to the pension system.

Companies and governments need to alter their retirement policies and benefits in order to not bankrupt themselves. Many organizations are moving from defined benefit pension plans to defined contribution plans to limit their liabilities. However, even with the changes, there's concern that current private and public pension systems cannot be sustained. Employers and governments need to rethink their strategies. The time to act is now, while there is still a large labour pool available.

As retirement age is decreasing, life expectancy is increasing, which means that the length of retirement is growing longer. The result is that a growing number of older persons will be supported for longer than ever by a shrinking younger population.

Retirement will remain very popular even for the workaholic boomers. They're an active cohort and will find plenty to do. Many will launch second careers. If they can afford to retire, they will. There needs to be an incentive for them to stay.

Trend nine: return to work from retirement

Those who retire early often reconsider their decision and return to the workforce. Statistics Canada reports that nearly 69% of people who retired between the ages of 50 and 54 went back to work within

---

12. Leroy Stone, *New Frontiers of Research on Retirement,* Statistics Canada, Catalogue No. 75–511–XPE (2006).

two years. Of those who retired between the ages of 55 and 59, 39% returned to work. Only 6% of those 65-plus continue working.

Many are looking for an opportunity to contribute that doesn't necessarily mean they have to work 70 hours a week, or even 40.

Trend ten: phased retirement

Which leads us to—phased retirement. Phased retirement is a relatively new concept that appeals to workers who want to reduce their workload but don't want to retire completely. Phased retirement offers a full-time employee the chance to work on a part-time basis, whether it is fewer hours a day, fewer days a week or fewer weeks a year.

Organizations benefit by retaining the mature employee's wealth of experience, knowledge of procedures, industry knowledge, customer service skills and technical skills sets, while the employee continues to enjoy the social and financial benefits of being part of the workforce. This option will be appealing on many fronts as mature workers face retirement.

Danger Zone: Structural Problems Facing Organizations

The demographic workplace trends identified in Chapter Two present real dangers for organizations that have not analyzed the implications for their future business operations. Those blithely conducting business as usual may be about to sail over a precipice.

Employers pay a great deal of attention to current market pressures and demands, as they should. Unfortunately, they are not paying equal attention to the strategic opportunities and dangers represented by our rapidly changing workforce. In just five short years, organizations will be on the brink of that aforementioned precipice—the coming workforce shortage. Leaders need to devote time and resources now to develop ways to avoid a potentially disastrous fall.

Here are four key structural problems in organizations that could undermine future success.

Lack of strategic planning

Today's lean organizations are so busy tending to day-to-day operations that there's no time or manpower available for strategic planning. What strategic planning exists is confined to individual job functions or departmental needs. Corporate downsizing over the past two decades has resulted in organizations becoming reactive, not proactive, to workforce pressures. They move from crisis to crisis, devoting all their time to putting out fires instead of finding ways to fireproof themselves. How can they do otherwise when their staff is already spread thin? To plan for the coming talent shortages, organizations need to designate people to research, think and strategize. Designing creative strategies takes time, but in today's marketplace, time is money and there is none available to invest in strategic thinking. This short-sighted approach must change if organizations are to remain competitive.

It is a CEO's responsibility to make sure that his or her organization takes the time to plan and to invest capital into developing innovative policies and programs to attract, retain and motivate employees and thus avoid the coming workforce crisis.

CEOs should be asking their human resource professionals to explain the organizational lay of the land. They should also share the organization's goals and strategies with HR. This information exchange will provide the foundation for any forward planning within the organization with regard to the skills and talents needed in the coming decade. Let's face it, it's impossible for organizations to know if a crisis is imminent if they don't match business goals to the skills and experience they possess, or need to possess, to achieve those goals.

The first step for any organization is to understand the unique workforce demographics in each of its business functions—for example, IT, sales, administrative and research divisions. Second, it's vital to be clear about what functions are critical to the organization's continued growth and success, and what skills and talents will be needed in the next five and 10 years to meet strategic business objectives.

Productivity

Companies constantly strive to improve productivity. This can be achieved in several ways. One of the easiest for management is the cut-and-slash method—that is, to cut staff, increase the number of work hours for remaining employees, and slash employee benefits. This does indeed reduce costs and force employees to work longer and harder, but it does not increase the productivity of individual employees in the long term. Not to mention that it is not sustainable for the health of workers, either.

Time and again we hear that employers downsize their 50-plus workers, whom they view as expensive, only to replace them with two or three younger workers. Output decreased, hence the need for the additional staff. The younger workers are certainly paid less but contribute only a portion of the skills that the 50-plus worker did and require more of the manager's time. This is not an increase in productivity unless the organization is specifically looking to change organizational goals.

Another method of increasing productivity is to increase employee engagement. This is not easy to achieve but the benefits are substantial for the organization. Watson Wyatt and other organizational consulting firms demonstrate through their global workforce studies that employees who are the most engaged are also the most productive. These studies also reveal that organizations with the best shareholder value have employees who are highly engaged.[13]

Boston College recently undertook a survey of employer attitudes to 50-plus workers and found that they are generally perceived to be more productive than younger workers but more costly. The survey asked employers how various characteristics affected the productivity of older workers. The two characteristics most frequently cited as advantageous for both white-collar and rank-and-file workers were: "knowledge of procedures and other aspects of the job" (precisely what the psychological literature cites

---

13.   Watson Wyatt, *Staying @ Work*, 2005.

as the strength of older employees), and "the ability to interact with customers," (consistent with many anecdotal conversations about the capabilities of mature workers). The least advantageous characteristic for perception of productivity of 50-plus workers was employer "expectations for how much longer workers will be working," which, as this publication will discuss later, has profound implications in actual hiring decisions.[14]

When employers expect that mature workers will leave them, it affects employer perception of the 50-plus worker value. This means that the thought of having an employee leave in a short period of time can be a deterrent to hiring—even though we know that 50-plus workers are most likely to stay with their present employers due to their loyalty.

Interestingly, the OECD reported that France's productivity increased 2.32% between 1996 and 2002, compared with 1.44% for the rest of the EU, when that country reduced its work week from 39 hours to 35.[15] The hope of the French government was to increase the number of workers by 10%, but instead, in many workplaces employers negotiated more time off for the workers and increased their productivity! Workers were motivated to work harder to get more time off.

Engagement

On the inside cover of this book is the engagement model that employers can use to benchmark their ability to be an employer of choice for 50-plus workers. These criteria will be discussed in detail in Chapter Six.

Engagement means employees have a positive attitude towards the company's products and/or services and what the organization

---

14. Alicia H. Munnell, Steven A. Sass, and Mauricio Soto, "Employer attitudes to older workers: Survey results," Boston College, *Issues in Brief*, 2006.

15. Stephen Clarke, *Talk to the Snail: Ten Commandments for Understanding the French* (Toronto: Viking Canada, 2006), 32–33.

is trying to achieve. Engaged employees believe their employer has their best interests at heart. As a result, these individuals will go above and beyond their job descriptions to collaborate with others in attaining organizational goals.

It is well established in several studies by many different academic institutions and organizational consulting firms that engagement is the best way to tell if a worker has a transactional and meaningful relationship with an employer. It is also known that mature workers are more satisfied with their work, and therefore more engaged, than younger workers. Unfortunately, many employers seem unaware of these facts and therefore fail to capitalize on what 50-plus workers bring to the workplace.[16]

Engaging a workforce takes time. Building an organizational culture that truly values employees requires a strategic approach over a three-to five-year period. There are no shortcuts, and all employees and managers need to be involved.

Employers who are able to engage their workforce will also increase productivity, customer satisfaction and employee satisfaction, and meet organizational goals. Organizations that harness the power of the engaged 50-plus demographic will have a built-in competitive advantage.

Workforce shortages

Organizations are letting employees go in both thoughtful and reckless ways. When the goal is to bring down fixed costs by cutting workers, the approach is often to target those who are more experienced and older or, in unionized environments, those nearing retirement. The rationale is that younger, cheaper and less experienced employees can easily replace older, expensive and experienced employees.

16.   J. Harter, T. Hayes, F. Schmidt, "Business Unit Level Relationship Between Employee Satisfaction, Employee Engagement and Business Outcomes: A Meta Analysis," *Journal of Applied Psychology*, Vol. 87 No. 2 (2002): 268–279.

But when the dust settles after cutbacks and businesses try to plan for growth rather than consolidation, skills gaps in the remaining workforce cause the organization to stumble on the road to implementing its strategies. Time and time again we hear stories about organizations that suddenly develop huge credibility gaps with consumers because of customer service issues.

The health care sector: the Seven Oaks Hospital model

Look at the health care sector. Canada doesn't have enough doctors and nurses. Our universities are not graduating enough medical professionals and licensing bodies are not allowing those trained in other countries to practice here. We are not meeting the growing demands of our communities. Why not, when we've known about this problem since the early 1990s? Surely there's been a plan put in place to correct this alarming situation? Obviously not, since nowhere in Canada are there thousands of students working towards a career in medicine.

Those nurses we do have are leaving the profession in droves. There are several reasons, including physically demanding work that results in musculoskeletal injuries, lack of respect in the workplace, shift work, poor morale and poor pay. Call me crazy, but it seems to me that we should be doing everything we can to keep our nurses and other medical professionals on the job, as the demand for medical services increases in lockstep with our aging population.

Seven Oaks Hospital in Winnipeg is a shining example of a medical facility trying to retain experienced medical personnel as a way of dealing with workforce shortages. Management has worked to help employees stay healthy by offering wellness, rehabilitation and other services onsite, services of particular benefit to shift workers who might have difficulties accessing these services outside usual working hours. As a result, Seven Oaks has the best retention record of any hospital in Manitoba.

Lack of skilled tradespeople: the Orkin PCO solution

Other sectors are also experiencing a critical shortage of specialized tradespeople. Fewer young people are opting for careers in the trades and experienced workers are retiring by the thousands. Businesses like Orkin PCO, Canada's largest pest control company, are coming up with their own solutions. Orkin helped establish a program at an Ontario college to train exterminators, but the program folded due to low admissions. Undeterred, Orkin came up with a new strategy that takes advantage of existing human resources in its 50-plus demographic. Orkin now counts on its own long-term technicians to train and mentor young people interested in a career in the pest control industry.

Many CEOs are losing sleep over how their organizations will overcome labour shortages. Depending on the type of business, those shortages may require recruiting more low-skilled labourers or highly skilled specialists. Alternatively, the solution may involve retaining experts in key areas, as well as those with in-depth, broadly-based or irreplaceable organizational knowledge.

One thing is clear. In the coming years organizations will need to factor the undervalued 50-plus demographic into any workforce shortage solution.

The disconnect between Human Resources, CEOs and managers

Survey after survey shows that organizations are aware of the coming demographic changes but that few are actually doing anything about the situation. A recent Ontario survey of HR professionals asked about their awareness of the coming change, and what movement towards solutions with a 50-plus demographic had occurred. More than one-third of respondents were aware of the issues, half were concerned—and only 18% were doing something about it.[17]

Yet when CEOs were surveyed by Ipsos Reid[18] in 2005, they consistently listed "attracting and retaining workers as the workforce ages" as one of their top five concerns. What's going on? If HR managers and CEOs are concerned about attracting and retaining workers as the workforce ages, then why isn't it happening? The reality is that most organizations suffer from a disconnection between CEOs and HR professionals. They may both perceive the impending danger of a workforce crisis but there are no strategies to work jointly towards minimizing the risks to the organization.

Many HR professionals have related to this author how difficult it has been to convince managers to broaden their viewpoint regarding whom they should hire. Each manager seems to need to undergo a personal epiphany where he or she "discovers" that mature workers fit the job requirements as well, if not better, than younger workers. Managers have a paradigm in their minds about why certain individuals they've hired in the past have been successful. Many instinctively hire in their own likeness, instead of focussing on the specific skill sets needed for a job. For example, financial managers tend to look at financial stereotypes, such as employees earning more the longer they're with the organization. But as employees gain more experience they also become more effective and therefore more productive. The costs of benefits associated with 50-plus employees do go up, as some begin to experience age-related health issues. But with rising rates of diabetes, cardiovascular illness and other chronic conditions in younger people, benefit costs for employees of all ages are expected to skyrocket in the coming years. However, organizations often assume that only the older worker demographic is driving the costs upwards. Old paradigms must be challenged for workplace change to occur.

---

17. Marjorie Armstrong Stassen, "Human Resource Strategies for Older Workers," *HR Professional* (2004), 43–47.

18

After hiring a number of 50-plus workers, one manufacturing firm experienced great resistance from their middle managers, who voiced concerns that mature workers would be slower, more difficult to manage and experience more injuries. Corporate resistance continued for two years as the managers continued to prefer younger hires, despite having to constantly train new younger workers because of high turnover rates. Only when HR was able to prove that older hires stayed with the company longer, had fewer injuries, a strong work ethic and weren't difficult to manage, compared to their younger colleagues, did the resisting managers change their tune and welcome 50-plus workers.

The coming workforce skills shortage crisis will require a well-thought-out and unified strategy at every corporate level. HR professionals, CEOs and managers all need to communicate more effectively with each other if organizations are to survive and prosper through the next business decade.

CHAPTER 4

Current Human Resource Issues and the 50-Plus Demographic

The need for total health

Businesses currently pay about half of employee health costs. They do this through hospital, health and drug costs, and by paying for paramedical costs that provincial governments no longer pay. When you add short– and long-term disability, Workers Compensation premiums, and absenteeism costs to the list, it becomes clear that organizations are in fact footing much more of the health bill. As stated earlier, these costs are skyrocketing.

Yet employers invest very little in keeping workers healthy. Little is done to help employees reduce health risks caused by poor lifestyle choices such as obesity, lack of exercise, poor eating habits, high cholesterol and substance abuse. It's hardly surprising that chronic conditions such as diabetes, heart disease and cancer will continue to rise, as will the associated costs of treating them.

The World Health Organization defines health as "a complete state of physical, mental and social well being and not merely the absence of disease. Health is a resource for everyday life, not the object of living. It is a positive concept emphasizing social and personal resources as well as physical capabilities."

"The term "**total health**" refers to physical, mental and social health. The effect of physical health issues on employer costs has already been discussed. But **mental health issues**, with their precursors of stress, anxiety, lack of work-life balance and interpersonal and family pressures, also have profound effects on productivity and financial costs for organizations. The effects are seen in absenteeism, presenteeism, (a term used by economists to refer to those employees who are at work but because of a medical condition, are not really functioning—in other words, the working sick), burnout and depression. Mental health issues can also lead to physical illness, further compounding the problem.

These health issues translate into approximately $2000 for every health risk.

Social health refers to relationships within and outside of the workplace. These are the relationships that nurture us as social creatures, whether they are with our spouses, immediate or extended family members, friends, coworkers, or managers. Employee assistance program statistics show there's a complex relationship between professional responsibilities, workplace relationships, supervisor support, family support and employee resiliency.

Some employers find that focussing on employee wellness and health programs makes a difference to employee functioning and their productivity. They bring in nurses to take cholesterol, blood pressure, body mass indexes and other readings to determine people's health risks. They then offer programs to support employees in reducing their risks, like personal coaching, nutritional counselling, smoking cessation programs and gym membership discounts, to name a few.

Those 50-plus are acutely aware of their health and the effects their lifestyle has on it. Some workers are in denial, some don't care and will continue to indulge in risky lifestyle behaviours, but the vast majority want to stay at least as healthy as they are. Those who do get a taste of feeling better after making lifestyle changes begin to understand that they can control their physical health and the effort often becomes self-reinforcing.

Mature workers have usually figured out how to stay mentally healthy—except of course when life throws them a curve ball and they need to cope with one of the major life stressors of death of a loved one, divorce, job loss or major illness.

Fifty-plus employees, with their lifetime of experience in negotiating relationship issues, usually fare better than younger workers on social health issues and with their sharp eye for fairness are quick to notice when things don't ring true. This ability to understand underlying problems can make them useful observers of organizational systems and can be tapped as a resource by astute managers. Understanding relationships can also make 50-plus workers great with customer and client interactions.

Pensions

At the 2006 Summit on the Mature Workforce, Louise Greig, a lawyer from Osler, Hoskin Harcourt LLP, told attendees that pension plan structures are too rigid for changing workforce realities. Many plans not only prevent organizations from rehiring retired employees but also discourage retirees from re-entering the workplace. Organizations need to ensure that their pension plan pays people for their best five years, not their last five years. There are regulatory obstacles to phased retirement as well as to pension benefits and taxes.

Employers need to think about what they are trying to achieve with their pension plan, and then tailor the product to create the desired outcome, or outcomes. For example, if retaining senior employees and persuading them not to retire early is important, offer a defined benefit plan.

A **defined benefit plan** promises the participant a specific monthly benefit at retirement and may state this as an exact dollar amount. Monthly benefits could also be calculated through a formula that considers a participant's salary and service. A participant is generally not required to make contributions in a private sector fund, but most public sector funds do require employee contributions. Unlike defined contribution plans, the participant is not required to make investment decisions. Employers with defined benefit pension plans also tend to place a relatively low value on the productivity of mature workers. This is hardly surprising, as these plans are often used to induce mature workers to retire.

A **defined contribution plan** provides an individual account for each participant. The benefits are based on the amount contributed and are also affected by income level, expenses, gains and losses in the underlying investment. Some examples of defined contribution plans include employee stock-ownership plans and profit-sharing plans.

Many organizations are already moving from defined benefit plans to defined contribution plans, thus shifting the responsibility for managing the financial risk of retirement to the employee.

Other plans are bankrupting the companies that developed them. Take General Motors with its generous pension plan, for example. GM is being forced to restructure its entire pension system.

Current benefits, pensions and taxes are major impediments to retaining workers of retirement age that are mainly controlled at the federal and provincial level. Until the federal and provincial governments step in to open up options for employers and workers, all stakeholders will be penalized. Employers will have limited access to 65-plus workers. Workers nearing retirement age will have limited choices for employment and the federal and provincial governments will have less revenue available from taxes from both organizations and workers.

Phased retirement should be a very popular option but it's not. With the current regulatory structure workers lose any early retirement subsidies that would otherwise be available. Benefits must be drawn in the form of a lump sum amount. Members prefer monthly payments and the amount of income that can be drawn is relatively low, and in most cases insufficient to replace the lost income. These factors make phased retirement an unattractive option even in jurisdictions where it is permitted.

According to Greig, it is impossible to design one pension plan that fits all worker needs. The variables of salary, the pension formula, the length of pensionable service of the worker and if the employer would offer an unreduced pension earlier are all factors.

"The major options now are for employees to retire from their current employer and work for another organization or retire and work for their previous organization. The main options for employers who want to retain workers are to reduce an employee's hours but provide an enhanced salary and continue pension accrual."[19]

Employers may want to retain certain workers key to their business goals. They need flexibility to attract these workers by offering pensions that they can continue to build on. Employees, on the other hand, need flexibility to continue earning pension credits part-time and preferably portable ones.

Forward-thinking organizations like Merck Frosst, three-time winner of a *Best Employers Award for 50 Plus Canadians™*, has found a way to offer its workers an additional retirement savings plan tax free, (over and above the regular RRSP option available to all Canadians) through some innovative work with Revenue Canada. Employers are currently looking for their own solutions to help employees have enough funds for their retirement.

---

19.   Louise Greig, Osler, Hoskin & Harcourt LLP, "Recent Developments in Canadian Laws Affecting Mature Workers," speech at the 2006 Summit on the Mature Workforce, Toronto.

Benefits

Organizations pay for about 50% of employee health costs through their benefit plans. These benefit costs are rising annually at a rate of 8%–20%, depending on what is included in the definition of benefits. The bulk of many organizations' benefit expenditures—70% to 80%—are drug costs, once short-term and long-term disability drug costs are factored in. Therefore, the more illness or disease experienced by employees, the more the organization pays out.

Benefits do not always provide adequate support to 50-plus workers, as they are often capped at a certain amount. And the types of drugs allowed onto an insurance formulary can mean the difference between some employees being able to function or not. Some drugs for chronic or catastrophic illness are not on any formularies and can bankrupt an individual, making it impossible for them to retire.

Paramedical services—chiropractic, naturopathic, physio-therapy, and massage therapy—are often minimally funded by benefit plans that only allow for three to four visits per employee per year. These amounts usually do not support the full cost of treatment and both the employee and employer pay. The employee may not be able to afford to pay personally for more treatment and often lets active treatment lapse. The employer then ends up paying more when the employee needs to take days off due to illness. Sometimes the employee, if not properly treated, may resort to medication to control symptoms without curing the problem. Yet these paramedical services support employee health and often make all the difference to an individual's engagement and productivity. They are particularly important to the 50-plus worker in terms of maintaining wellness.

The Catholic Children's Aid Society of Toronto noticed that its overall benefit costs began to go down when it increased the paramedical service limits, allowing employees to complete preven-tative treatment and hence return to their former health.

Seven Oaks Hospital also focused on keeping its staff healthy through the use of onsite fitness facilities, physiotherapy and internal specialists, providing the support in hospital to give shift-workers better access and save other employees from having to travel offsite for health appointments.

Flexo Products offers a free assessment from a chiropractor who became Flexo's ergonomics specialist in its manufacturing environment. Employees took up the offer of the free assessment and were shown exercises to keep them limber; those who had vulnerabilities were shown how to strengthen those areas of their bodies. Further visits to the chiropractor were then claimed through their benefits. The majority of the workforce is male and to have this access onsite meant that many who had just suffered with their muscle strains now had solutions offered that worked. Flexo Products experienced a drop in short-term disability claims and incidental absenteeism.

Forward-thinking organizations will need to adjust their benefit plans to better accommodate and attract the growing 50-plus demographic.

Human Resource practices

HR practices can be part of the problem or part of the solution in creating a supportive work environment for the 50-plus employee.

The number-one request of 50-plus workers is more **flexibility** in how and when they do their jobs (see Demand for alternative work arrangements).

The second is that they be treated with **respect and fairness**. This means offering career development experiences, promotions and equal opportunities to *all* employees. Many workplaces are unintentionally discriminatory toward 50-plus workers, due to the organizational culture and the lack of understanding by human resources staff about the importance of mature workers to their organization, and what the needs of those mature workers are.

Age bias is insidious within organizations and permeates many of their systems. It exhibits itself when for example, a recruiter interviews a mature person for a job and poses questions such as, "Where do you see yourself in five to 10 years?" This is appropriate for someone just starting out or in mid-career, not someone who may be focusing on helping an organization work towards *its* goals by contributing a lifetime of knowledge.

Managers inadvertently display the same biases to the myths about 50-plus and younger workers. They often request younger workers as hires, seeing them as more likely to stay (false: younger workers job hop about every two years), less likely to get hurt (false: older worker experience prevents them from putting themselves in risky situations) more malleable (maybe: though perhaps "gullible" is the word; 50-plus workers are just as able to change but may need rational explanations and questions answered).

HR needs to support making organizations more diverse to reflect both customers and demographics. To many, diversity simply means a workplace that is open to women, the disabled and visible minorities. But smart organizations are beginning to change their culture by **adding age into the diversity mix**. Direct Energy is one employer that is doing just that, with great success. The company is giving both its mature employees and its HR professionals the opportunity to address the needs of the 50-plus worker.

Mature workers need less supervision because they're familiar with workplace expectations and exercise judgement on the job. They ask questions when they aren't familiar with a situation and generally work safely. Take Flexo Products. They found that when mature workers were introduced to the workforce, their accident and injury rates went down. This had a dramatic effect on the productivity of their small organization.

Demand for alternative work arrangements

Implementing alternative work arrangements to attract and retain 50-plus employees is not as difficult as it may initially seem. Excell Services operates a call centre in Penticton, B.C. and offers its employees the ability to customize their work schedules. This enables them to work shifts which allow them to pursue other activities or fulfill other obligations.

Overwhelmingly, workers of all ages want flexible work options. There are a number of alternative work arrangements that appeal to the 50-plus worker: early start and finish times, job sharing, compressed work weeks, telework, weekend-only work, and seasonal work.

Start and finish earlier

Beginning work at five or six a.m. is often appealing to those who may be early risers, or who no longer have young children at home. Some employees with young children also like this option, as it allows them to juggle parenting responsibilities. Starting at seven a.m. and leaving at three p.m. allows a parent to be home at the same time children get out of school.

Job sharing

Two people sharing one job can be an appealing option when a full-time employee wants to reduce his or her hours, but the employer needs someone in that position on a full-time basis. Job sharing is often an alternative proposed to management on an as-needed basis, but this idea could be utilized more fully in the future to meet organizational needs in a talent drought.

Compressed workweek

Compressed workweeks are becoming increasingly popular, especially during the summer months. Employees work 12-hour shifts for 10 days or two weeks, then enjoy several days off in a row, or add an hour or two to their day in order to take Friday off. The former is already common practice for police officers, fire fighters, nurses and oil rig workers, to name but a few. This option is attractive to workers wanting to pursue other interests or responsibilities, or those forced to work away from their home in order to take advantage of economic opportunity.

Telework

Working from home is ideal for workers who may not want to commute, or who want or need to be closer to home for other reasons. Direct Energy and Metasoft Services are two companies who have invested in technology that allows many of their staff to work from a home office.

Weekend-only work

Some people may be interested in only working on weekends because of commitments to family, friends, their own businesses or other jobs. Employers may find the extra staff useful on high-volume weekend days. It's a win-win alternative.

Seasonal work

Seasonal work gives employees the opportunity to go on leave for extended periods of time while maintaining benefit eligibility, an ideal option for snowbirds. Toronto Auto Auctions of Milton, Ontario, RBC Global Banking Service Centre and the City of Calgary all offer this type of flexibility to their employees.

Turnover and retention

Turnover is a big issue in today's complex and multifaceted workplaces. Managers are dealing with four distinct generations, as well as employees from a wide variety of cultures. Managing an increasingly diverse workforce requires interpersonal skills seldom taught in business schools and an understanding of how to motivate each group.

Research has shown that younger employees establishing a career will generally stay with employers for shorter periods of time and jump more often from job to job, compared to their 50-plus colleagues. Younger workers also tend to be less loyal and less committed to the organization than older employees.

Turnover costs organizations a tremendous amount in lost knowledge, business continuity, productivity and business growth. Are the high value or key employees leaving your organization because of dissatisfaction? As the war for talent heats up, organizations simply won't be able afford high turnover rates in the 50-plus demographic. Especially since the proportion of the 50-plus workforce will be significant and increasing.

Loss of knowledge within the organization

The loss of critical knowledge as senior employees retire can seriously affect day-to-day business. In the five years prior to 9/11, intelligence-gathering organizations in the U.S. shed half their employees, most of whom were highly experienced personnel. This short-sighted strategy greatly diminished the agencies' abilities to interpret information and led to the intelligence community's failure to pick up clues about the coming terrorist attacks. While not all examples are this dramatic, knowledge loss can lead to serious business failures and customer service issues. Increasingly, organizations are closing down because of a lack of skills and knowledge needed to support the business.

From an employee perspective, organizational knowledge consists of three separate parts.

Individual knowledge is the knowledge, skills, and experience an individual brings to the job, and what he or she has learned over time within the organization.

Social knowledge is how an employee gets things done and ensures that tasks meet business goals. In most organizations, a how-to operations manual can only go so far. A great deal of individual decision-making takes place as services and solutions are customized for individual customers. Therefore, there may be many variations on how to solve a problem or meet a need depending on individual customer requirements. Social knowledge also includes an individual's relationships with colleagues and the ability to create new solutions through collaboration.

Structural knowledge is a thorough understanding of the policies, practices and systems that have been created within the organization and industry over the years.

All three kinds of knowledge abound in the 50-plus demographic. The depth and breadth of their individual and collective knowledge is a valuable resource for the savvy organization that supports its mature workers.

Statistics Canada is doing an excellent job of building a culture where individual learning is expected and continuous. All workers learn early how to come together for projects and social knowledge is built over the projects and years. Statistics Canada makes line managers responsible for their employees' development, and work by committee to refine and increase the expectations of all members of Statistics Canada. This is one organization that is great at measuring their outcomes and quantifying expectations. This makes Statistics Canada flexible and ready for the changing priorities of government and their impact on human resources.

Recruiting practices

Organizations tend to discount the experience that 50-plus workers possess, as well as their contribution to creating more efficient, productive organizations, often through several downsizings. It's often not until a manager has let a mature employee go, then tried to fill that position, that he or she realizes it will take two or three new hires to meet the requirements of the job as it now exists. Organizations have this experience time and time again.

How often do you hear hiring managers say that the applicant pool was good but not outstanding? This implies that they hired a good candidate, not a great one. Often there are great candidates who have the talent and experience the employer wants but the recruiter or manager is more concerned about the applicant's age.

Mandatory retirement

Alberta, British Columbia, P.E.I., and Nova Scotia prohibit mandatory retirement. Mandatory retirement no longer makes sense—not when we're already struggling to find skills in a dramatically shrinking workforce and have a healthy older population interested in, and capable of, working.

There is no evidence that tossing older people out of the workforce at 65 creates jobs for younger workers (a favourite rationale for mandatory retirement). What does increase the labour pool is a strategy of training and retraining workers. The training alternative also increases staff motivation and commitment for all employees, while decreasing recruiting costs, encouraging competition for jobs, controlling labour costs and increasing choice and productivity. Such a strategy can only be beneficial for organizations in every sector.

Merck Frosst does a wonderful job of giving its workers the opportunity to be challenged by new jobs projects and secondments. It is constantly looking within to fill positions and workers often cross disciplines to work in new areas of the business. This leads to a very engaged workforce at Merck Frosst.

Excell Services (who specifically located in a retirement community to take advantage of the 50-plus worker pool) finds that 50-plus applicants who have never turned on a computer can learn to use one, as well as other complex technology. They may take longer to train, but these mature workers become every bit as productive as their younger counterparts.

Employee engagement surveys show that many 50-plus employees are eager to be challenged and appreciate the opportunity to learn and grow in their careers.[20]

20   James K. Harter, Theodore L. Hayes, Frank L. Schmidt, "Business Unit Level Relationship Between Employee Satisfaction, Employee Engagement and Business Outcomes Meta Analysis, *Journal of Applied Psychology, Vol.* 87 No. 2 (2002): 268–279.

Organizational culture

All organizations want to be employers of choice. They want to be able to attract the best talent to meet their present and future business goals. They want broad experience, maturity and an ability to move swiftly to meet the needs of their market.

The corporate downsizings of the last two decades have resulted in companies doing more work with less staff. This means employees have to work harder and faster and that speed has, by necessity, replaced quality of service. But when RBC Global Banking Service Centre surveyed their customers about the quality and speed of services, they found that their customers did not want to sacrifice quality of service for the sake of speed. Hence speed is something that is not necessarily valued by customers as much as by employers. Employers need to assess what their customers really want. Running a lean organization may keep operating costs down, but at what price?

Fifty-plus workers add experience, stability, corporate knowledge, ability to train newer workers, mentor others and be mentored and want to see their employer succeed. Employers who level the playing field find that they can unleash the efforts of the 50-plus worker to their organization's benefit. Employers time and again express surprise at how grounded their workplace becomes and how morale increases with the addition of 50-plus workers. In the immortal words of Rodney Dangerfield, all 50-plus workers want is a little respect!

CHAPTER 5

The Perfect Storm —Preparing Your Organization for the Workforce Crisis

Every few years, another buzzword makes the rounds, a hot idea that usually has little organizational impact other than to create more work for HR professionals. The latest HR catchphrase is "workforce planning" but this time smart organizations are taking the issue very, very seriously—for good reason.

Our workforce is aging and our talent pool is shrinking rapidly. Without careful, strategic planning, organizations may find themselves embroiled in a savage war for talent, unable to fill key positions or stem the flow of knowledge loss.

Over the next 20 years, almost 10 million Canadians will be leaving the workforce, taking their years of experience and knowledge with them. These are the ubiquitous baby boomers, those born during the two decades following WWII. Boomers currently make up a third or more of the nation's workforce, and many are in the most skilled and senior jobs. By 2011, the first wave of boomers will turn 65; by 2025, one quarter of our entire over-16 population will be at retirement age.

The loss of millions of workers is one thing. Not being able to fill their shoes is something else again. It's a simple case of demographics—boomers are the largest generation in history and there won't be enough younger, skilled individuals available to fill the void. Canada's healthcare, construction, energy, oil and mining sectors are already being squeezed by a labour and skills shortage that will only intensify in coming years, according to a recent Deloitte survey.[21] Of the 55 organizations questioned by Deloitte, 80% said that a shortage of talent is already limiting their productivity and efficiency. Further, 67% of respondents identified attracting specific types of labour as their most critical people challenge.

Yet only 18% of organizations have strategies to deal with impending workforce shortages.[22]

"This situation shouldn't be a surprise to anyone," says Kevin Aselstine, Managing Principal at Towers Perrin. "We just might end up in what I call 'the perfect storm,' where we're facing a demographic crunch and its impact on the labour supply at the same time that human capital is becoming more important in implementing dominant business strategies."

Workforce planning

"Simply stated, workforce planning is the process of ensuring that the right people are in the right place, and at the right time, to accomplish the mission of the organization," says Janis Sugar, Manager of Sales and Marketing at Manpower. "A workforce plan

---

21. Deloitte, *Managing Talent Flow: 2006 Energy & Resources Talent Pulse Survey Report*, 2006.

22. Deloitte.

translates strategic thinking into concrete action in the area of staffing and training needs."

The workforce planning process

Many organizations, both public and private, have developed models for workforce planning. Putting aside variations in terminology, the processes are all very much alike. All rely on:

- an analysis of present workforce competencies
- an identification of competencies needed in the future
- a comparison of the present workforce to future needs to identify competency gaps and surpluses
- the preparation of plans for building the workforce needed in the future
- an evaluation process to assure that the workforce competency model remains valid and that objectives are being met.

While this process is simple in outline, it depends on rigorous and comprehensive analysis of the organization's work, workforce, and strategic direction.

One organization already involved in such a thorough self-analysis is Telus Corporation, a telecommunications company whose operations are centred in Alberta and British Columbia.

"Part of our business strategy for each of the business units that make up Telus is to examine the skills we'll need three years from today," says Josh Blair, Senior Vice-President of Human Resources Strategy and Business Support. "We're constantly assessing employee demographics and attrition rates to determine what that means in terms of hiring and development over the next three years."

Calgary-based companies like Telus currently lead the way in workforce planning. They have no choice. The province has the hottest economy in the country and is already experiencing a talent crunch in many sectors, forcing employers to compete for qualified workers.

Six strategies for workforce planning

What exactly can organizations—of any size—incorporate into their own workforce planning models? Here are some ideas courtesy of Manpower's *Confronting the Coming Talent Crunch: What's Next?* [23]

1. Encourage prolonged working life

Hanging on to older and long-term employees will be vital in the talent-scarce future. Mature workers, especially those in key positions, often have irreplaceable skills, experience and corporate and industry knowledge. Organizations need to find ways to encourage their 50-plus employees to stay on, and to lure retired workers back. Fostering an inclusive culture is a start. Offering training, development and promotion on merit, not age, flexible hours, working from home, less time-consuming roles, contract and consultancy work and mentoring opportunities are just some of the ways companies can attract and retain mature talent critical to their success.

Workplaces that try to get a "balance" in all their age groups will soon see that this kind of assumption is folly, if organizations hope to compete with those who promote a workforce that reflects current demographics. In other words, if the current population is 30% boomer, employers should maintain a workforce that is 30% from that demographic.

2. Make flexible use of available talent

Create your own internal pool of "understudies" by encouraging cross-training and labour flexibility. Moreover, organizations can introduce more temporary, contract, consultant and outsourced talent to their workforce to accommodate variability in demand.

---

23.   Manpower, *Confronting the Coming Talent Crunch: What's Next?* A Manpower White Paper, 2006.

3. Invest in training and development

While many organizations view training and development as a reward, or avoid it as too expensive, companies actively planning for the future are investing in the training and retraining of their workforce.

Employers need to do all they can to retain potentially useful and adaptable talent, whatever their current role in the organization. They no longer have the luxury of laying off 5,000 employees with obsolete skills one day, and hiring 5,000 people with the right skills the next. Organizations are finding that when they go looking for the workers who will fill their needs, they aren't there any more. One strategy is to consider training employees who skills are or will become obsolete to allow them to fill upcoming requirements. Another is simply to train from within. Take the example of Direct Energy, who is retraining retail staff from HVAC retail stores to become HVAC technicians when they close their retail operations. These 50-plus workers know the Direct Energy culture, plus they are a known employment entity to Direct Energy and are poised to continue to contribute to Direct Energy's goals.

4. Hone attraction and retention approaches

The war for talent is on! The best and the brightest candidates will be able to pick and choose among employers, so it's up to organizations to make themselves an employer of choice. This means offering workers motivating opportunities for varied experience, good prospects for promotion, great working conditions and benefits, and an organizational culture that fosters a healthy work-life balance.

To know what drives attraction and retention in your industry, the first step is to do some employee research. Do you have the right mix of incentives? Do you need to fine-tune learning or career development opportunities? What are the things that are important to your target groups?

At Telus, for example, the one-size-fits-all benefits plan most companies offer employees has been shelved, in favour of a more flexible package that meets the needs of workers of different ages and with different skills sets.

You don't have to remodel your entire workforce—that could be too daunting and confusing. Instead, look at the skillsets of employee groups that are critical to the delivery of your business strategy—your engineers, your product development staff—and plan your attraction and retention strategies accordingly.

Becoming an employer of choice also means creating and sustaining a culture of equality and inclusivity where women, 50-plus workers, people with disabilities and minorities are represented and believe they have equal access to career development opportunities.

5. Enhance links with schools

Employers need to establish links with schools and educational institutions that generate meaningful work-placement opportunities, ones that give students a true taste of real work skills and prepare them for eventual employment. This is also a great way to attract the best and brightest before they even graduate.

If your company needs 50 additional research engineers in the next three years but the schools in Alberta are only producing two or three a year, then you need to cast a wider net—beyond the province and beyond our borders. Maybe you should be working with Canadian colleges and universities to increase the number of people accepted into their engineering programs.

6. Tap into underemployed sources

It's not just 50-plus workers who face obstacles in procuring employment. There are other underutilized groups out there that organizations could mine for talent—for example, the disabled. According to Statistics Canada, 13% of working-age Canadians have some sort of disability and 56% of them are either unemployed or not in the labour force. Many of these people are highly educated and, with some accommodation, perfectly able to meet organizational requirements. These accommodations, such as Braille printers, assisted listening devices or reconfigured workspaces to allow for wheelchair access, are often quite simple and inexpensive. Many IT companies, including Microsoft, have been doing this for years.

As the old cliché goes, think outside the box. Your candidate has no Canadian experience? Who cares? There are thousands of highly skilled new Canadians who are ready and willing to work but whose qualifications do not meet Canadian requirements. Hire that Colombian-trained engineer in another capacity, support him or her in meeting Canadian standards and voilà! You have a loyal and much needed engineer.

"Consider the attitude, not the resume," advises Janis Sugar of Manpower. "Train young people with the right outlook in basic work skills and guide them to programs that will prepare them for the future."

Act now or lose big

All experts agree—the time to plan is now. In five years, when that first wave of boomers retires, it will simply be too late.

Shifting an organization, especially a larger organization, takes time. You need time to see if strategies work, and if they don't you need time to implement others. There's a saying that sums it all up: failure to plan is planning to fail.

Top 10 Talent Shortages in Canada[24]

1. Skilled Manual Trades
2. Sales Representatives
3. Customer Services Representaives/ Customer Support
4. Labourers
5. Drivers
6. Mechanics
7. Machinists/Machine Operators
8. Engineers
9. Management/Executives
10. Cleaners & Domestic Staff

24. Manpower Canada, 2007.

CHAPTER 6

The Workplace Institute Engagement Model for 50-Plus Workers™

It's just common sense: when an organization has a happy, engaged workforce, productivity is up, absenteeism and disability claims are down, customers are satisfied and business plans are more easily attained. But creating a happy, engaged workforce has its challenges.

On of the biggest difficulties facing employers is trying to engage a working population that is increasingly diverse, both culturally and generationally. Four distinct generations now make up our workforce: generation Y, generation X, baby boomers and veterans, each with its own culture, communication style and way of working. Given this diversity, there can be no one way of engaging and motivating today's employees. Instead, each company needs a multifaceted engagement model that can be adapted to meet the needs of its unique and changing organizational demographics.

In order to survive the coming talent crunch, employers need to develop age-specific policies and procedures to attract, motivate and retain their best workers—across all age groups. Until now efforts have been primarily geared towards younger workers, but it is the 50-plus workforce that needs particular attention if organizations are to unlock their potential.

It is important to remember that any changes to a corporate culture take time to implement. The strategies outlined below have proven successful for organizations proactive in engaging the 50-plus worker. Together these pillars provide an engagement model for other companies eager to activate this undervalued cohort.

WORKPLACE INSTITUTE
ENGAGEMENT MODEL FOR 50-PLUS WORKERS™

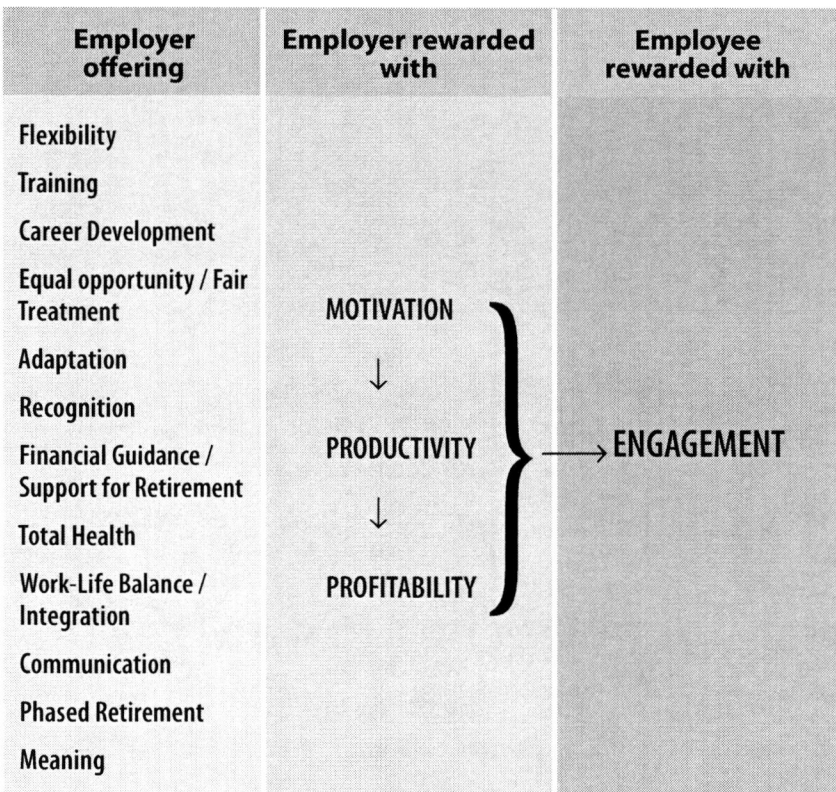

Employer offering	Employer rewarded with	Employee rewarded with
Flexibility		
Training		
Career Development		
Equal opportunity / Fair Treatment	MOTIVATION	
Adaptation	↓	
Recognition		
Financial Guidance / Support for Retirement	PRODUCTIVITY	ENGAGEMENT
Total Health	↓	
Work-Life Balance / Integration	PROFITABILITY	
Communication		
Phased Retirement		
Meaning		

Flexibility

When 50-plus workers weigh whether to join, remain with or rejoin an organization, one of their top three considerations is flexible work arrangements. Many younger workers will also appreciate having the option to work in non-traditional ways. Those organizations that listen to their employees, understand their needs and find ways to accommodate those needs through flexible work options will be rewarded. They will experience less turnover, less absenteeism, higher morale, greater loyalty and a willingness on the part of all employees to go the extra mile to reach corporate goals.

As discussed in Chapter Four, these work arrangements include:

- flex time
- job sharing
- compressed work weeks
- telework
- weekend-only work
- seasonal work
- paid or unpaid leaves of absence or sabbaticals.

Metasoft Systems in Vancouver, Halifax and St. John's allow their workers to work from home, flex their time, shorten their week, or make their own suggestions on how best they can meet their organizational goals. Those in St. John's often start their day at 6 a.m. in order to talk with their U.K. nonprofit prospects and customers in the morning. With the time distance working in their favour, at 6 a.m. they can be talking to their U.K. customers at 11 a.m. British time and be in direct contact a good part of their day.

Some organizations find flexible benefits that employees can tailor to their own needs to be useful. Direct Energy offers full-time and part-time staff a flexible benefit account, and an opportunity for pro-rated benefits to those who may be phasing their retirement or are interested only in part-time hours. To attract mature workers Direct Energy pays health care premiums and provides a $1400 per year flexible spending account to retired employees with no age limit.

Equal opportunity/fair treatment

Most organizations proudly display their mandates and mission statements on their websites and pretty well all of them contain phrases such as "treat all employees with respect," and "conduct business in a fair and transparent manner." But many older workers would tell a different tale. These mature workers, with their low absenteeism rates and solid work ethic, are often ignored by managers and see their younger counterparts receive preferential treatment regarding training, career development and promotion opportunities. Job postings often include youth-oriented code words such as "flexible," "energetic" and "fresh." Any 50-plus worker knows applying for such jobs will be a waste of time.

Why are mature employees not treated fairly? Generally because they're victims of many stereotypes, most of which are untrue. Current stereotypes portray 50-plus workers as being rigid and inflexible, expensive, difficult to train, scared of new technology, less productive and not as energetic or as enthusiastic as younger workers. The reverse is the usually the reality.

Even in times of business downturns or corporate takeovers, it's often younger workers who are redeployed, while mature workers are given the stark choice of being laid off, let go or accepting early retirement packages, regardless of their past and present performance. It's considered easier and less messy to focus on older workers when downsizing.

Fair treatment includes equal access to training and promotions. While most organizations would never wantonly discriminate on the basis of an individual's race, religion, gender or culture, many concentrate their career development programs on younger workers. One of those myths about older employees is that they'll retire as soon as possible; it's a waste to invest precious resources into further training or to promote them to key positions. In fact, most mature workers still aspire to achieve, learn and develop and have no intention of leaving their field of expertise. If forced into retirement, they often continue working as consultants or launch their own businesses.

Fair treatment means not excluding older people from corporate activities by focussing on events for younger workers. Fair treatment means extending benefits to workers beyond the age of 65. While mandatory retirement has been eliminated in many provinces, employers are not legally required to extend disability and other benefits to workers over 65. Neither are 65-plus workers entitled to Workers' Compensation coverage. Fair treatment does not end at some predetermined age.

Training

One popular stereotype of older workers is that they are just hanging in until retirement, hopefully an early retirement. So why bother training them? Older employees will indeed exit early, if they feel shut out of any further training opportunities.

Another factor to weigh when considering who gets training is turnover. Younger workers have higher turnover rates than older workers, so concentrating training on those under 40 is not cost-effective. According to the U.S. Bureau of Labor Statistics, workers 45–54 stayed on the job twice as long as those 25–34.

A lot of statistics are bandied about as to when employees from various industries will be "eligible to retire." "Eligible to retire" is not "intend to retire." Organizations need to begin asking workers what their intentions are and what it will take to make them stay.

Think about it. Invest in a 25-year-old who in all likelihood will leave the company within five years and take the knowledge gained through your training programs to a competitor? Or invest in a 50-year-old, and gain a long-term commitment of another 10, 20 or 25 years?

Another stereotype is that older workers are resistant to new technologies and difficult to train. Again, this is simply not true. Studies have shown only a negligible loss of cognitive function for those under 70. While older workers sometimes do take longer to absorb completely new material, their better study habits and accumulated experience actually lower training costs. Excell

Services found that those in the 50-plus age group took somewhat longer to train for the job, but once trained on computers this group was every bit as effective as younger employees. Another interesting fact that Excell discovered was that it was better to train workers with similar skill levels together rather than putting neophytes with trainees who were very comfortable with computers.

Are mature workers technophobic? Older individuals may not be playing video games or downloading tunes onto their iPods, but the 50-plus are proving their ability to embrace technology by being the fastest growing group of Internet users.

What can be done to make training accessible to all employees? Begin by posting training opportunities, instead of relying on word of mouth or manager recommendations. Training should also be available throughout an employee's working career, whether the worker is 25 or 65.

Toronto Auto Auctions found that it had outgrown its informal hiring practice and needed to post all jobs in order to get the word out to their whole organization.

Home Depot has a formalized training program and milestones that employees must achieve in their learning of the job. They utilize online e-learning that encourages an environment of continuous learning.

Companies also need to remove barriers to training opportunities, such as ensuring that employees working outside the office under flexible work arrangements or in remote locations have the same access and same consideration as their head-office colleagues.

At Direct Energy a mobile training unit is brought to employee sites in smaller locations to provide training onsite. The company has also received government approval to use its more senior employees to provide training within authorized apprenticeship programs.

At Orkin PCO Pest Control technicians were no longer being trained at community colleges—so Orkin reached out to its senior technicians to train willing younger employees.

At both Direct Energy and the Catholic Children's Aid Society of Toronto, work-related tuition is reimbursed 100%, while non-work-related tuition is reimbursed 50%.

Training strategies should not be focussed just on employees; training can be used to dispel the myths and stereotypes that plague all workforce groups. Managers need to be trained on how to create a fair and equitable workplace, and to understand the strengths and talents both young and not-so-young workers bring to the table. The Workplace Institute knows that educating managers on the value of 50-plus workers is effective in changing their behaviour.

Last but not least, smart companies use training to preserve corporate knowledge and plan for succession. Many forward-looking organizations have established knowledge transfer processes to harness the decades of skill, experience and industry knowledge held by their senior, long-term and mature employees. These include mentoring programs, succession-planning initiatives and video and audio libraries. In this way, when key employees do decide to retire, their knowledge remains and their successors are ready to step up to the plate.

Statistics Canada is further along on this curve that most organizations. Its sophisticated multidisciplinary committees from all areas of operations concentrate on continual training, cross-operational secondment opportunities and project work.

Career development

Another sure way to lose skilled mature workers is to deny them access to promotions and other career development opportunities, such as secondments to special projects. An exclusionary policy is corporate suicide in industries already scrambling for engineers, scientists and other highly skilled workers. Today's healthy 50-year-olds can expect another 20 to 30 years of active employment. The secret is making it worth their while to stay.

Promoting on merit, not age, is the first step. Being seen as an employer that, like Merck Frosst, trains, develops and promotes on ability alone will not only attract and retain 50-plus workers, but will reduce turnover rates among younger workers. No one wants a career that peaks at 45. Organizations should expect their employees to continue developing skills and abilities throughout their employment and workers should expect the opportunities to do so.

Savvy employers provide career coaching to interested employees and have internal initiatives in place to help people develop career paths. One of the most effective ways to plot career paths and determine appropriate career development and promotional opportunities is through a performance review process that stresses future growth as well as past performance.

Home Depot has formal performance development reviews twice a year that focus on continuously challenging employees to develop their skills and competencies.

Career development includes mentoring the next generation of executives. The only way to do that is to retain mature, highly skilled workers for as long as possible. Many senior individuals will delay retirement, or come out of retirement, if offered the opportunity to pass on their knowledge to promising younger individuals. For many at the end of their career, the chance to give something back to an organization or industry is more important and more attractive than title and salary. It's the chance to create a legacy.

Merck Frosst has a well developed mentoring program as does Statistics Canada.

Direct Energy continues to look creatively at their 50-plus workers and tries to engage them in areas that may be of interest to them and helpful to the organizational goals through their performance development process, but also through communicating innovation across their operational silos.

Adaptation

Working takes its toll on us all. The corporate mergers and downsizings of the past two decades have resulted in many workers doing the job of two or three people, which means long hours and greater stress. Technological advances may have improved workflow but have also created new forms of injury and disability. White-collar workers of all ages are suffering from shoulder, neck and back pain, carpal tunnel syndrome, eyestrain and headaches caused by those longs hours in front of a computer. Blackberries, e-mail, cell phones and laptops mean many are connected to work 24 hours a day, seven days a week.

For physically demanding professions like nursing and construction, musculoskeletal injuries are an occupational hazard. Add age-related physical limitations such as arthritis and diminishing eyesight and hearing, and remember that in five years, more than half our workforce will be over 40. That's a lot of people working with pain and discomfort.

Organizations need to adapt their environments to meet the physical needs of their workers. Interestingly, a worker-friendly environment is one of the top draws for both older and younger workers. Well-designed, ergonomic workspaces, good lighting, headsets and the ability to take frequent breaks to reduce strain will become increasingly important.

Home Depot has adapted their workplace design to have the shelves stacked at night to avoid daytime employees needing to worry about keeping the shelves filled, allowing them to focus on helping customers. This also means that there are specialized jobs that cut down on safety and injury issues.

An environmental redesign includes adapting the delivery of training programs to meet the needs of different groups. For 50-plus workers, this may mean well-lit, quiet rooms and disseminating information in smaller units.

Excell Services find that workstations that are totally flexible, allowing people to sit or stand when they perform their call centre duties, provide the adaptation necessary for many people.

To retain older, key employees, job parameters need to be redesigned. After many years with one company, highly competent individuals often accumulate dozens of responsibilities. The result is frustration, exhaustion, burnout and an early departure. Companies need to strip away unnecessary functions from these employees and allow them to concentrate on the vital, key areas that support corporate objectives.

Policies and procedures need to be rewritten to ensure opportunity is based on ability, not age, and that any transgressions will be dealt with in the same manner as discrimination based on gender, race, religion, culture or country of origin. One positive way of encouraging this is to tie manager performance bonuses to reasonable expectations of hiring and retention of 50-plus workers.

Seven Oaks General Hospital has built adaptation into its organizational culture in order to retain all employees, but especially their nurses, who are so crucial to running a hospital, by supporting their health through a variety of innovative methods. In terms of work design, for example, nurses are taught to strengthen vulnerable muscles to avoid injury, and specialized equipment has been introduced to assisting in lifting tasks.

Recognition

The number-one factor that will persuade mature workers to stay on the job or come out of retirement is almost certainly the knowledge that they are valued and appreciated by an organization.

This goes far beyond traditional long-term service awards, although such celebrations are important. Recognition means being promoted on merit and having equal access to career development and training opportunities. It means age is no consideration in the hiring process and that older individuals are regularly recruited.

The Royal Bank Global Banking Service Centre recognizes the value of its long-term staff by recruiting employees with specific skills who are about to retire from other areas of the bank. Once these employees retire, they are hired back on a contract basis at GBSC. The City of Calgary has created what they call a "rehirement" program whereby retired managers are hired back to support succession planning initiatives, as well as a retiree pool that allows interested retired municipal workers to return for temporary employment opportunities when they arise.

Other organizations like Merck Frosst recognize the value of their long-term, highly skilled employees by inviting them to mentor younger employees, lead special projects, develop training programs and speak at industry conferences.

Metasoft Systems offers recognition for long service as well as presents at different years, such as a trip to Las Vegas after five years and an Alaskan cruise after 10 years.

At the Catholic Children's Aid Society of Toronto, employees begin receiving $525 annually at their 10-year anniversary. After 20 years of service, employees receive a bonus of an additional one week vacation, which increases every five years until after 40 years (!) they get an additional 5 weeks vacation.

Annual recognition dinners are also a popular way of celebrating and acknowledging employee commitment and contribution.

Financial guidance

To successfully recruit and retain skilled older workers, programs need to be created specifically for them. This includes financial guidance and support in preparing for retirement.

It's amazing how many people simply don't think about retirement and assume their pensions will sustain them and their partners for the 20, 30 or even 40 years they will not be working. But as employers begin to pass the onus for future financial stability back to their employees, it is increasingly important for employees to understand the implications and how to prepare for their retirement.

There are many ways for an organization to deliver this important benefit. Financial counselling through workshops and seminars, RRSP contribution programs, company shares, allowing older employees to "top up" their corporate pension plan by making extra lump-sum payments, tax shelters and investment advice are all attractive offerings and an inducement to the 50-plus workforce.

Merck Frosst has created a flexible benefits program that can adapt to the changing needs of its employees, specifically those who at 50 encounter changing family circumstances, such as the need for dependent or spousal support. One such initiative is what Merck Frosst calls the Savings Plus Account. This is separate from RRSPs and offers Merck employees the added advantage of further tax deductions while helping them continue to save toward their retirement. Almost 25% of contributors are 50-plus employees.

Allowing employees to participate in an employee-share-purchase plan, as Direct Energy does, can be another way to let workers save.

The Catholic Children's Aid Society of Toronto has begun offering retirement planning to 50-plus employees, with their partners. They are assisted by a formal program along with a Retiree Mentorship Program where people who have already retired offer their experience about how to avoid pitfalls to those currently planning for retirement.

Health support

Myth time again. You've probably heard that older workers are not as healthy as their younger coworkers and use more medications, therefore costing company health plans more money. Well, this claim is both true and false. Many health conditions are age-related, such as Type 2 diabetes, hypertension and heart disease, but it's not so much age as poor lifestyle choices over a long period of time that tend to result in these conditions. With millions of employees all hitting middle age at the same time, many of whom are paying the price of a sedentary lifestyle, it's no wonder the health care system is sagging under the strain.

But health costs are also rising because more and more young people are also developing these so-called age-related (or what should be called lifestyle-related) conditions. The incidence of Type 2 diabetes is skyrocketing in younger and younger people, thanks to ever-increasing rates of obesity. Doctors are now beginning to see even teenagers and children manifesting signs of the disease. So we can't blame just the boomers for increased health costs.

What is certain is that as we age, we are subject to diminished hearing and eyesight, arthritis, prostate problems, and other associated annoyances. So yes, older people are more likely to need eyeglasses, hearing aids and some medications. And if they have abused their bodies through poor lifestyle choices, middle age is when they will develop chronic health problems. By and large, though, baby boomers are pretty healthy.

In addition to the financial demand on the health system of millions of workers all hitting middle age at the same time, rising drug costs have also contributed to the health cost problem. Medical technology has created newer and better drugs to control many chronic conditions and these new drugs are expensive.

The one way to reduce these health costs while still supporting employees is through prevention and alternative health care.

The good news is that workers and organizations who implement these strategies begin reversing poor health immediately and workers begin to feel better than they have in years, which is very gratifying and self-motivating.

The way to begin is by finding out what conditions—and what health risks—most affect a particular workforce. This can be done through individual health-risk assessments of employees, overall assessment of the organizational benefit usage and current management practices. For example, is the workforce mostly male or female? What is the average age? What programs are they accessing most? Is a good percentage overweight? What prescription drugs are being charged to the company's benefit plan? Lets say the organization finds its employee demographic is mostly males who tend to be, on average, 35, slightly overweight and not active. Health prevention programs targeting heart health, prostate health, weight control and exercise could be launched to improve the general health of this demographic.

Understanding how to use data concerning drugs, short– and long-term disabilities, EAP utilizations, absenteeism, and insurance claims will help a company get a handle on the present and future health of its employees. We know that preventative health and wellness programs improve the health of a company's workforce and reduce the cost of benefits.

Offering comprehensive health coverage is attractive to 50-plus workers, especially if it includes catastrophic drug coverage. These medications are often not covered and can bankrupt an employee. It would also be wise to include health plan coverage for alternative health care, such as massage therapy and chiropractic services, to help control current physical and mental health problems and reduce the chance of certain conditions worsening.

Flexo Products has done just this, by arranging for a chiropractor to visit its facility once a week. In addition to providing acute care, the company chiropractor also assesses new employees to determine if any part of their body needs strengthening in order to prevent future injury.

Organizations are also beginning to equip buildings with defibrillators and train several volunteers on how to use the equipment. These measures have saved lives of fellow workers. Statistics Canada and many other workplaces now invest in this lifesaving equipment.

Today's employees also need support for mental and social health issues. These include stress management, eldercare issues, parenting, resiliency training and relationship issues, both personal and professional. An employee assistance program is essential to help deal with the multitude of issues facing workers of all ages, but especially the complex needs of the 50-plus.

Employees should also be educated on the value of critical care insurance in supporting employees and their families if their health takes a turn for the worse. Critical care insurances offers lump-sum payments that can be used for specialized treatment or support for the individual or family. As well, disability insurance is invaluable for employees who may be working as contractors and need an income replacement source while they rehabilitate.

Direct Energy provides a short term disability program that gives all employees financial security in case of illness or injury away from work. This program allows for 120 days of sick pay. Employees have the option to receive cash back by reducing coverage to 50% or 80% according to their own lifestyles. There are several options on how to use the extra cash, such as increasing their savings in the Group Retirement Plan.

Does it work? The Catholic Children's Aid Society of Toronto is very focused on educating employees about the precursors to ill health and supporting them in staying healthy. CCAS offers a wide range of work-life, wellness and paramedical supports such as chiropractic, naturopathic, massage, physiotherapy, and nutrition services. This focus on health support has led to a decrease in drug claims as a percentage of overall claims, mostly due an increased utilization of paramedical services. The CCAS paramedical benefits are quite generous, allowing an employee to continue with a thera-peutic program to a successful outcome, instead of having a $200 or $300 cap on such services, as is the norm.

Work-life balance/integration

Mature workers are at the top of their game. They've established their careers, raised families and are now turning their attention to traveling, community involvement, hobbies, social engagements and spending time with family. The baby boomers are, after all, the most active generation in history and retirement is generally a dirty word for them. They don't mind aging, but they have no intention of getting old. The boomers continue to want it all.

So let them have it. Retaining key mature employees or rehiring highly qualified retired workers means encouraging an active professional life and personal life as well. Organizations can do this in many ways. For example, they can offer sabbaticals so individuals can fulfil volunteer commitments, flex-time options, working only part of the year to allow for travelling, or support employees' charitable work through corporate donations.

Extended caregiving responsibilities need to be accommodated for the 50-plus workforce. Many boomers who delayed starting families are also part of what is called the "sandwich" generation, caught between caring for children and caring for elderly relatives. Older boomers may be the primary caregiver for an ailing spouse. Therefore, eldercare support through an EAP and flexible work arrangements can mean the difference between retaining an employee and losing them to full-time caregiving responsibilities.

At Direct Energy extra flex-benefit dollars can be used to obtain additional vacation days. This benefits those 50-plus who are interested in working after retirement or plan to reduce work prior to retirement.

Communication

Companies can provide a variety of programs and policies to attract and retain mature workers. But these offerings are useless if workers know nothing about them. It's essential that organizations effectively communicate their attraction, retention and engagement initiatives to their target audiences. These communications should include *why* the employer offers such programs so that everyone in the organization understands that mature workers are respected, valued and essential to the business.

The Catholic Children's Aid Society of Toronto makes sure employees understand their benefits in detail and makes a point of educating them to ensure that there is good uptake for those employees who need the various types of health support.

Ensure that when you communicate an innovative change that you also explain the reasons for the change so employees do not misinterpret the reasons. The City of Calgary's treatment of its long-term planning commissioner (discussed below under Retirement) is a good example of how to do this right.

Policies regarding age discrimination and equal access to career development, training and promotions need to be written and distributed to all staff. They should also be prominent on corporate publications and websites.

Training and career development opportunities must also be disseminated throughout the organization.

Several organizations like Excell Services, Direct Energy and CCAS all have "refer a friend" programs with financial incentives to recruiting employees after the new hire has stayed in the new job for a period of time.

Finally, communicate through action that the company is walking the walk, not just talking the talk. Let staff know that individuals are hired and promoted on merit alone—by doing so. People should see that mature employees are not just long-term staff members but new hires as well. All employees should know of the company's succession planning and mentoring initiatives. They should understand these have been established to capture the remarkable knowledge and talents of older workers, and that this experience is too valuable to be lost.

Merck Frosst, Excell Services, Toronto Auto Auctions, Direct Energy and Statistics Canada all have employee advisory councils that bring forward suggestions for change in the workplace. These organizations find the councils valuable in bring to management's attention changes that are needed to support 50-plus workers.

Phased retirement

Retirement doesn't have to mean cold turkey—working one day and not working the next. Many people would love to test the waters. Research has shown that a large percentage of retirees return to the workforce within two years. They miss the social interaction, mental stimulation and personal satisfaction of being employed.

One appealing way to hang on to key employees is to offer them phased retirement options where they can reduce their hours or their responsibilities.

The planning commissioner of the City of Calgary had been a municipal employee since Calgary was little more than a town. When he announced his decision to retire, senior management went into shock because he'd been involved with city planning for so many years and had an irreplaceable understanding of his department's history. Many in the municipality relied on his knowledge and guidance and there was great trepidation about whether his decades of experience could be preserved and passed on to new leaders. In discussions with the outgoing planning commissioner, senior management discovered that workload, not a desire to stop working, was the key factor in his retirement decision.

Taking a long-sighted strategic approach, management decided to divide his job into three new positions and move the commissioner horizontally into a less-demanding role so that he could mentor his replacements. A communication was sent to all city employees explaining what was happening and why. The announcement made it clear the commissioner was not being eased or pushed out of his position, and that it was a case of capturing his valuable knowledge and persuading him to postpone his retirement. This stopped any speculation in its tracks and reflected the depth of respect the city had for the commissioner's knowledge, reputation and commitment.

Direct Energy gives Unionized Home Services technicians two additional weeks of vacation in their retirement year.

Meaning

Employees are looking for meaning in their work. This can come in a variety of forms: feeling good that they are contributing to the success of an organization, training younger or newer employees on the job, forming relationships and acknowledging the social aspect of work, or believing in the mission of the organization or what they do for communities.

Take Home Depot. When disaster strikes a community, or when something in the community needs to be built, Home Depot provides its employees as well as materials to do good works and help the community.

Actions and programs that employees identify with, and that support personal or community principles, add value to employment and contribute to engagement. If the organization is involved in a activity that employees want to support, such as helping children, or nonprofits find foundation dollars for causes employees believe in, as Metasoft Systems does, all parties become winners.

Become an employer of choice for the 50-plus workforce

Experienced workers are watching. They've seen large organizations send their senior and long-term staff packing at the first sign of a business downturn, or in the event of a merger. Workers of all ages will not stay with an employer who operates in a discriminatory manner toward older, experienced workers. Instead, they'll seek workplaces that value and respect knowledge and experience. As boomers increasingly become part of the mature workforce they will continue to be a force to be reckoned with and pressure the workplace to respond to their changing needs. Organizations who work hard to develop policies and practices to engage, attract, motivate and retain the 50-plus workforce will reap the benefits in the coming labour shortage. Companies who ignore and disrespect older workers do so at their own risk. Using the *Workplace Institute Engagement Model for 50-Plus Workers™* will help organizations get on the right path.

7

The *Best Employers Award for 50 Plus Canadians*™

Since 2004 the Workplace Institute, with the support of its partners, has put out the call to organizations to apply for the *Best Employers Award for 50 Plus Canadians*™. The award is designed to recognize and reward innovative and effective programs or initiatives that lead the way in establishing best practices with 50-plus workers while achieving organizational goals.

Our goal: new best practices for all 50-plus workers

We are interested in celebrating and sharing "good news stories," the ways organizations have introduced or tried new ideas or programs with 50-plus employees and reaped rewards for the individuals, teams or organization. Organizations benchmark themselves against others and receive feedback on ways to improve. We seek to raise the bar of excellence through groundbreaking, inventive or novel approaches to addressing workplace issues with 50-plus workers.

Awards Categories

We are searching for great practices in the categories of:
- career development
- retention
- recruitment
- workplace culture/practices
- management practices
- health—mental, social, physical
- retirement/retiree practices
- benefits
- pensions.

Developing new ways to retain and attract 50-plus employees is now a priority for smart organizations seeking to establish themselves as employers of choice in a competitive labour market. Organization or team stories and solutions form the basis for these great practices.

Eligibility Criteria

The winners are all from workplaces with more than 10 employees and from all sectors—private, not-for-profit, academic institutions, labour organizations and governments. The application may come from one or more business sections within an organization in the case of organizations that are larger or multifaceted, where an individual unit within the organization may have created something unique within the organization.

Evaluation

Not all workplaces are outstanding in every area. The objective is to find organizations that may be doing one great thing to meet the needs of their older workforce **in one category,** or many little things **in several categories** that incrementally add up to make it a great place to work for the 50-plus employee.

Winners were evaluated on the criteria of:

- program/idea/initiative description
- rationale
- responsiveness to needs of the people or organization
- innovation
- quality
- effectiveness of the initiative, as measured by positive change and measurable results.

Completed applications were scored by an independent panel of judges with experience in labour, business and human resources.

The Winners

Best Employers Award for 50 Plus Canadians™ 2007

Catholic Children's Aid Society of Toronto
Direct Energy
Excell Services
Flexo Products
Merck Frosst
Metasoft Systems
Seven Oaks Hospital
Statistics Canada
Toronto Auto Auctions

Best Employers Award for 50 Plus Canadians™ 2006

Carrier Truck Centres
Catholic Children's Aid Society of Toronto
City of Calgary
Direct Energy
Excell Services
Flexo Products
Seven Oaks Hospital
Home Instead Senior Care
Merck Frosst
Orkin PCO Services
Toronto Auto Auctions

Best Employers Award for 50 Plus Canadians™ 2005

Avis Rent a Car
Home Depot
Merck Frosst
RBC Global Banking Service Centre

Avis Rent A Car System, Inc.

Address	1 Convair Drive East Etobicoke, ON M9W 6Z9
Telephone	416-213-4278
Fax	416-213-8632
Website	www.avls.ca
Type of business	Transportation
Canadian locations	163
Total employees	1361
2005 Award categories	Recruitment Workplace culture Retirement /retiree practices

The company

Avis had a costly business problem with transporting its cars and discovered that the competencies of 50-plus workers matched with its need to improve its operations.

Avis Rent A Car System, LLC and its subsidiaries operate one of the world's leading car rental brands, providing business and leisure customers with a wide range of services at more than 2,000 locations in the United States, Canada, Australia, New Zealand, Latin America and the Caribbean region. Avis is one of the world's top brands for customer loyalty, ranking as the number-one car rental company in the Brand Keys® Customer Loyalty Index for the past eight years. The company is part of Avis Budget Group, Inc., (NYSE: CAR) formerly Cendant Corporation. Avis has employees located across Canada and received one of the first *Best Employers Award for 50 Plus Canadians™* in 2005.

The recruitment problem

As with any business, the ability to effectively and efficiently deliver products to customers is paramount. For car rental companies such as Avis Rent A Car, the task of shuttling a fleet of clean cars, dirty cars, damaged cars, cars needing service and cars that belong in another city or even another country, is a challenging one. Making this task even more difficult is the fact that customers tend to arrive and drop off their rentals at the same time of day and on the same days of the week.

Approximately 10 years ago, Avis realized that using car transports to move their fleet had become simply too expensive, too inflexible and too slow. Hence, the idea of greatly increasing their brigade of "shuttlers"—people who drive the rental cars from one location to another—was born, and the search for reliable, responsible and safe drivers was on.

The solution: 50-plus workers

In terms of job requirements, Avis discovered that attributes such as work ethic, dependability, flexibility, stability, responsibility and safe driving records matched perfectly with those of older individuals. In the early days of the shuttler program, Avis actively recruited this demographic by handing out flyers in malls, seniors centres and other locations where 50-plus workers congregate in order to find drivers. Avis also gave them the opportunity to provide input into organizing the work and then gave them the flexibility to meet their personal needs by tailoring schedules.

The idea and the success of the program took off. Avis now recruits through word of mouth and ads in seniors magazines and today employs over 700 shuttlers, greeters and expeditors nationally, almost 80% of whom are in the 50-plus age bracket.

Workplace culture

Shuttlers not only appreciate the social outlet, camaraderie and extra income the position provides, but the flexibility. They can be absent for extended periods—perfect for snowbirds flying south for the winter—or fit their work around other interests and commitments. In return, Avis gets a large, flexible and cost-effective workforce that accommodates their business and market peaks and valleys—including time of year, day of week and time of day. The company has also found that older drivers have less accidents and minimal, if any, speeding or traffic infractions. It's a win-win situation for both groups!

With a diverse range of backgrounds, including former executives, accountants, pastors, educators, veterans and tradesman, one might expect shuttlers to be a divided group. The reverse is the case. Personal bonds go far deeper than former career interests. Being able to relate to each other, discuss current events and provide support is at the heart of this group's cohesiveness.

Many shuttlers are not only actively involved in Avis operations, regularly participating in Health and Safety Committees, Employee Participation Groups and other initiatives; they are also involved in their communities doing volunteer work.

The success of the shuttler program is perhaps best summarized in the words of the shuttlers themselves who say, "Avis provides one of greatest opportunities for people our age"; "We enjoy coming to work"; and "Avis demonstrates a progressive attitude towards employing people over the age of 50."

Advancement

Avis provides the opportunity for advancement to a higher paying job with added responsibility if this is what the employee wishes

Employee satisfaction

Avis conducts an annual survey to measure employee satisfaction and elicit suggestions to improve the program and/or workplace. Regular workshop meetings are also conducted to ensure that Avis continues to be an employer of choice for workers of all ages and backgrounds.

Carrier Truck Centers Inc.

Address	6 Edmondson Street Brantford, ON N3T 5N3
Telephone	519-752-5431
Fax	519-752-0370
Website	www.carriertruck.com
Type of business	Transportation
Canadian locations	4
Total employees	270
2006 Award categories	Recruitment Retention Workplace culture Management practices Retirement/retiree practices

The company

In the trucking business there are serious labour shortages in every category from drivers to mechanics. Carrier Trucks is an early adopter of recruiting and retaining 50-plus workers and encourages them to stay if they want to past the age of 65. This policy of respecting the talent and skills their 50-plus workers bring has enabled it to stay competitive as well as expand its labour pool.

Carrier Truck Centers Inc. operates four full service international dealerships along the 400-series highways in southwestern Ontario—Windsor, London, Woodstock, and Brantford. They sell new and used medium, heavy and severe service international trucks and each location offers parts and maintenance services.

Last year, Carrier Truck Center celebrated 45 years in business. Marvin Long became company president in 1967 and took the operation from one location with 25 employees to four locations with approximately 270 employees. Mr. Long is still active in Carrier Truck Center, but has turned control over to his son, Rob.

50-plus employees give Carrier the competitive edge

Marvin Long has always been a strong believer that if you are capable of doing the job then you deserve an opportunity to work for Carrier or continuing to work for Carrier. Rob Long holds those same values and the company employs 50-plus individuals in every job category, from mechanic to salesman to manager.

This philosophy has served the company well as it has become increasingly hard to find skilled mechanics. In fact, there is a serious shortage of trained mechanics, as fewer and fewer younger people are pursuing careers in the trades. This shortage will only worsen as hundreds of thousands of older tradespeople leave the workforce over the next few years. For companies such as Carrier Truck Center, it is difficult to find qualified mechanics of any age—as well as parts and sales staff.

To meet this challenge, Carrier Truck Center has the short-term goal of hiring additional qualified staff of any age and the long-term goal of retaining its workers and allowing them to work for as long as they are able and wish to do so. Carrier currently has 68 employees over the age of 50.

With you for the long haul: recruitment, retirement, advancement

At Carrier, qualifications and work ethic are what count. Age is not a consideration. In fact, the company recently hired a parts driver who is 57; one of their leading sales representatives is 76. Needless to say, there are no mandatory retirement policies at Carrier.

The company actively recruits older workers and has partnered with placement agencies allowing them the opportunity to bring forward qualified candidates regardless of age.

Through these practices, Carrier continues to make 50-plus employees feel welcome and appreciated. In return, Carrier has benefited from their years of experience and does not find older employees taking off time from work at the same pace as their younger counterparts.

"Our company motto is, 'We are with you for the long haul,'" says Carrier President Rob Long. "We have created a culture in which this motto not only applies to our customers, but to our employees. If they are able and willing to do the work, then we are able and willing to support them."

Catholic Children's Aid Society of Toronto

Address	26 Maitland Street Toronto, ON M4Y 1 C6
Telephone	416-395-1658
Fax	416-395-1551
Website	www.ccas.toronto.on.ca
Type of business	Government agency
Toronto locations	10
Total employees	600
2006, 2007 Award categories	Retention Recruitment Career development Workplace culture Management practices Retirement/retiree practices Benefits Other-Recognition

The organization

The Catholic Children's Aid Society (CCAS) of Toronto is a progressive workplace that leads the way with its HR practices. Specifically, it is breaking new ground in the areas of supporting employees who need expensive catastrophic drugs whose cost would otherwise decimate retirement savings; supporting wellness through expanding the access to paramedical benefits; and helping employees plan for their retirement by providing educational seminars on financial and lifestyle planning.

The Society is mandated to provide protective services to Catholic children seven days a week, 24 hours a day. One of four mandated child protection agencies in Toronto, it is funded and regulated by the Ministry of Children and Youth Service and is part of an Ontario-wide network of 53 agencies working to protect children from neglect and physical, sexual and emotional abuse.

CCAS is one of the largest child protection agencies in Canada, and fields a workforce of almost 600 employees as well as hundreds of volunteers, foster families and adoptive parents, many of whom are older than 50.

The Catholic Children's Aid Society of Toronto has been recognized for its progressive workplace through a number of awards. It has been named one of Canada's Top 100 Employers, as featured in *Maclean's* Magazine. CCAS was named in 2006 as one of Canada's Top 10 Employers in five other categories: Family Friendly Workplace, Promotion of Women, Promotion of Visible Minorities, Vacation and Time Off and Experienced Workers. *Today's Parent* also named CCAS as one of the Top 10 Family Friendly Employers 2007. This is the third consecutive year that the Society has won these awards. CCAS was featured in the *Toronto Star* and named as one of Greater Toronto's Top 50 Employers 2007.

Workplace culture

The majority of CCAS employees are Child Protection Workers responsible for the investigation and assessment of children in need of protection, provision of ongoing services to children and families and for acting as the "legal guardian" of children in care. In addition, there are front-line workers responsible for the adoption and placement of children in foster homes, group homes or outside resources. Providing support are Health Specialists, Parent Support Workers, Social Service Assistants, Child Care Workers, lawyers, law clerks, psychologists, consulting physicians and psychiatrists, as well as administrative, operational, professional, technological, finance and human resources staff.

Eighty-four percent of CCAS workers are female and 27% are older than 50.

The Society has a number of policies that address workplace culture, such as Expectations of Employees, Code of Ethics, Equity Policy, and Confidentiality, Harassment and Discrimination Policy. These policies have resulted in a positive management philosophy and harassment-free workplace.

High turnover and burnout: recruitment and retention lessons

Child welfare is notorious for its high turnover rate. People often leave within two years because of job demands. The retention of older, experienced staff is essential for CCAS to provide continuity, stability and wisdom in a stressful environment.

The Society has made staff retention a priority since 2000. In 2001, a retention study revealed that staff would stay long-term if certain conditions could be met. They wanted to continue to make a difference and contribute to society; learn and grow and be challenged; and at the same time have time off to relax and take care of family and self. As a result, a number of changes in the workplace were introduced to encourage staff retention across the Society and improve recruitment.

Child welfare is also a field with a high risk of burnout. Stressful aspects of the job include heavy caseloads, frequent court appearances, paperwork and accountability requirements, unpredictable hours of work, public scrutiny, low salary (in comparison to other professions), the complexity and responsibility of the child protection role and personal safety.

From 2001 to 2004, the Society increased the child protection staff complement by 64% due to an increase in caseload volume. This required a number of recruitment strategies. Experienced, long-term employees were asked to assist with this endeavour by recommending potential candidates for vacancies. For each successful referral, the staff member received $500. When new employees were hired, older staff provided role-modeling to younger workers in how to be successful in child welfare.

The Society has enjoyed a 62% improvement in turnover during the past five years, from 9.5% in 2000 to 5.9% in 2005. The provincial average in 2005 was approximately 15%.

Rewards and recognition

CCAS has a comprehensive recognition program that includes an Annual Long Service Recognition Bonus for 10 years or more service. On their anniversary date each year, the employee receives $525.

For staff with long service of 20 or more years, a Recognition of Long Service Leave is provided (in addition to normal vacation entitlement) in the calendar year in which the service is completed. At 20 years, they receive one extra week; 25 years, two weeks; 30 years, three weeks; 35 years four weeks; and at 40 years of service, five weeks.

The Society also hosts an annual recognition dinner with awards for service in five-year increments, from 5–40 years, as well as honouring retirees. The majority of staff members recognized with over 20 years of service are more than 50 years old. Retirees are invited to return to the agency and celebrate with current staff.

In addition, the Society supports a number of celebrations and social events throughout the year to build and strengthen morale.

Career development

The Society is committed to professional excellence through on-the-job training and professional development. Training is provided through the competency-based program managed by the Ontario

Child Protection Training System, as well as a comprehensive plan for in-house and relevant external training opportunities.

CCAS implemented a new training model in 2003 to support new staff. The New Worker Training Program consists of one centralized supervisor responsible for new worker training and 5–10 branch-based coaches to provide onsite teaching, role modeling and support. This provides an excellent opportunity for experienced workers to share their knowledge. There are also opportunities for skills exchanges where long-term employees share their areas of expertise.

There is no age limit for secondments that can meet individual employee training/developmental needs or the Society's needs. CCAS subsidizes 100% of tuition for courses related to work.

The Society provides many other training initiatives for employees, which are often joint efforts with other children's aid societies and other relevant services outside of child welfare. Some of this training is mandatory for all employees and time is allotted for them to attend. In addition, the Society offers training in specialized knowledge, which more experienced employees may wish to acquire. This provision is aimed at both learning new knowledge and in helping employees continue their professional development, which helps them to further plan their careers.

Succession planning is yet another tool at CCAS that provides opportunities for people to mentor successors while ensuring that their work efforts and contributions are being left in good hands when they retire.

Healthy employees, healthier bottom line

The Society provides employees with a comprehensive benefit program that is fair, equitable, competitive, creative and responsive to increasingly diverse employee needs and yet is financially practical for the Society. The plan includes a catastrophic drug policy that covers employees who may need very expensive drugs that would not normally be covered by organizations and that often eat into mature workers' retirement savings.

CCAS believes that employees should take care of their health. Hence, they are very focused on educating employees about the precursors to ill health and supporting employees in staying healthy. They offer a wide range of work-life, wellness and paramedical supports such as chiropractic, acupuncture, naturopathic, massage, and physiotherapy coverage, plus nutrition, psychological and other counselling services to support the total health of employees. This focus on wellness is paying off with decreased costs for illness later on.

At CCAS, benefits are communicated and highlighted, which always results in greater usage. CCAS paramedical benefits are also quite generous. There is no annual limit on the number of different paramedical services an employee can access in any given year; therefore a member can continue with a program up to $750 for each practitioner per year, versus many other employer benefit plans whose maximum covers all paramedical services.

One surprising result of this coverage is that CCAS has enjoyed a decrease in drug claims as a percentage of overall claims as a direct result of increasing paramedical claims being made. Typically, drugs account for 70% to 75% of total health claims; however this trend has been decreasing at CCAS. Their benefits consultants expect the trend for drug costs to increase approximately 15% per annum. The Society's claiming patterns for drugs are well below this.

Retirement/retiree practices that keep links strong

CCAS has found that older workers have wisdom, experience, maturity and institutional memory. Many of its retirees have made themselves available to return to work when asked. The Society may have 4–10 retirees on staff at any given time, several of whom act as floaters to assist the Society in filling in gaps where needed. For those in their 50s who may be thinking about retirement, this year CCAS began offering a formal Retirement Education and Lifestyle Transition Planning Workshop, to help employees and their spouses develop a personal action plan to help prepare them for the next phase of life.

Pre-retirement

The Society offers a comprehensive pre-retirement package to assist staff in planning for lifestyle changes upon retirement. Membership in the Ontario Municipal Employees Retirement System (OMERS) is mandatory for all staff on commencement of employment. A voluntary Group Registered Retirement Saving Plan (RRSP) is available to all employees.

Currently, the normal retirement age is 65; however, employees who wish to work beyond this may have their employment extended by the Society for a period of up to one year at a time.

Post-retirement

It is the Society's policy to provide retirement benefits to all employees with 10 years or more of service who retire early and/or at the normal retirement age.

Retirees and employees who reach 10 years of service at CCAS automatically become associate members of the Ontario Public Service QCC (Quarter Century Club), which recognizes and honours long-term commitment, excellence and quality service among current employees and retirees of the Ontario public sector. Members receive additional medical insurance, out-of-country travel, home and auto insurance, travel discounts and quarterly newsletters with helpful tips from the QCC.

Retirees receive the Society's quarterly newsletter and are invited to attend the Society's Annual Long Service Recognition Event. On an ongoing basis, a number of retirees are asked to return to work part-time. Other retirees have opted to become volunteers of the Society and the Hope for Children Foundation.

The Retiree Mentorship Program, where retirees participate in retirement planning sessions for 50-plus employees and share their experiences, provides valuable information and assistance to staff who have not yet considered their own retirement options.

City of Calgary

Address	P.O. Box 2100, Stn. M Calgary, AB T2P 2M5
Telephone	403-268-4840
Fax	403-268-5246
Website	www.calgary.ca
Type of business	Government
Calgary locations	120+
Total employees	11,000
2006 Award categories	Recruitment Workplace culture Management practices Retirement/retiree practices

The organization

Calgary is now Canada's fourth largest city, with a population nearing one million. In the past decade it has become one of the fastest-growing and most prosperous cities in the country, as Alberta experiences an economic and population boom fuelled by rising demand for the province's oil and gas resources.

The City of Calgary municipal government has approximately 11,000 employees who provide more than 500 services to Calgarians. The City operates 24 hours a day, 365 days a year from 120 locations throughout the city.

The City works closely with the Province of Alberta, the Government of Canada and other municipalities, as well as local businesses, community groups and agencies, to fairly and effectively allocate and invest the resources available to the City.

Providing infrastructure for citizens entails ensuring transportation, both roads and public transportation; safe water supplies through wastewater and water treatment facilities; and solid waste management. The City also provides quality of life services to citizens through community services such as fire and emergency services, parks and recreation; planning for whole new communities and redevelopment plans for older communities. In addition, there is the business of generating and collecting taxes. The enabling services, such as information technology, communication, finance and human resource divisions, support the customer service businesses.

Boom time and the retirement bubble

Calgary faces an impending workforce dilemma. The rapidly growing economy and population requires more civic services and infrastructure, yet a growing number of employees are eligible for retirement over the next decade. Compounding that situation is the increasing competition for skilled people provincially and nationally.

Over the years the City of Calgary has been part of the western Canada "boom and bust" economy, resulting in expansion and shrinkage of municipal staff. This scenario has been managed through hiring of part-time, temporary and contract staff and retaining a static group of core employees that has increased over time. The City's hiring cycles of core staff mirror the "boom and bust" economic cycles. As a result, the City has a bulge of employees who are all due to retire between 2010–2016. In many cases two or three levels in the organization are eligible for retirement at the same time, which will leave large experience gaps within the organization. By 2015, more than 50% of City employees will be eligible to retire. The City has a special interest in retaining as many experienced employees as possible to retain institutional knowledge.

The City of Calgary conducted a great deal of research into its retirement bubble and found that most of its senior, critical positions were occupied by individuals aged 55–60. The research also showed that the existing pension plan, which capped contributions after 35 years of service, was an impediment for long-term employees. It only made sense to retire at this point, and they did. But the City's research showed that many employees intended to keep working after retirement, although because of the pension situation, not for the municipality.

Calgary needed new strategies to retain institutional knowledge. After consultation with its employees, it came up with a couple of innovative policies to both expand the labour pool and bridge the gap between a senior manager retiring and finding a suitable replacement.

The City introduced two new programs directed at retiring and retired personnel. The first was the Rehirement Policy. After individuals have retired from employment with the City, they can apply to become part of the retiree pool and be rehired on a part-time, seasonal, contract or backfill position. This program includes a special rehirement policy to increase the pool of available employees for ongoing or project work. This is a unique program that meets the needs of a unionized/management environment.

Rehirement

This program is a restricted policy designed to complement Succession Planning, retain intellectual capacity and increase the possibility of mentoring new employees. It is intended for "management exempt" employees only and plays a critical role when the organization is in a situation where there is no immediate successor for the retiree, no suitable candidate is ready to be promoted now or within the very near future or the manager can't immediately hire into the position. In order for the position to be suitable to implement the rehirement policy, the recruiter must have the express intent of bringing in a successor in the longer term, and retain the retiree for no longer than one year. In addition, the work must be driven by a corporate need.

The retiree pool

The second new program is the creation of a "retiree pool." Retiring managers willing to return in another capacity can submit their resumes to a database for part-time, seasonal, contract or backfill positions. "They know the public sector culture and can hit the ground running," says Joy Halverson, HR advisor to the City of Calgary. The goal is to provide temporary assistance for a work unit to ease the workload with minimum orientation and training. Rehires have an opportunity to continue to make a contribution to the organization with no negative impact on their pensions.

The City already has a number of other programs in place that support the "Rehirement Policy" and "retiree pool" initiatives. These include: Performance Management System; Compressed Work Week; Job Sharing, Part-Time work arrangements; Deferred Leave and Leaves of Absence; flexible hours; and Succession Planning.

A win-win situation

The "Rehirement Policy" and 'retiree pool' programs are successful from an organizational perspective because:
- there is the opportunity to pre-select candidates
- the candidate is a known quantity within the organization
- the candidate has the organizational knowledge and experience and will require minimal orientation and training
- backfilling for a person who is on a developmental assignment or a special project is easily accommodated

- a recruiting manager does not have to go through a lengthy recruitment process and probation period
- though a manager can't use the policy for a permanent hire, it does allow time to develop possible candidates for the position.

The "Rehirement Policy" and "retiree pool" concepts can benefit employees by:

- providing work hour flexibility and work-life balance.
- augmenting retirement income
- providing the opportunity to continue to utilize worker knowledge and skills and make a contribution.

The City of Calgary is the first municipal government in Canada to mplement these unique types of policies.

Direct Energy

Address	80 Allstate Parkway Toronto, ON L3R 6H3
Telephone	905-943-6463
Fax	905-943-6412
Website	www.directenergy.com
Type of business	Energy and services supplier
Canadian locations	3
Total employees	2000+
2006, 2007 Award categories	Recruitment Management practices Retention Benefits Retirement/retiree support Career development

The company

Direct Energy discovered an interesting phenomenon when reviewing its sales force performance. A higher percentage of employees in the 50-plus demographic were part of the "million-dollar club" (those selling over $1 million worth of services and products to customers) than their sales force colleagues. Direct Energy realized the link: many of its customers are older than 50 and are interested in being served by those in the same age bracket.

Direct Energy is the leading North American supplier of energy and related services. Direct Energy is the master brand, with sub-brands operating in individual markets. The company provides natural gas and electricity plans along with a broad suite of products and services to support wise energy use, conservation and home improvement to both residential customers and small commercial businesses.

Direct Energy has benefited from recognizing the advantages of a 50-plus workforce in a number of ways, and tailored its policies to actively recruit within this demographic, maximize their effectiveness through supportive training and programs, and retain them with flexible career options.

Recruitment of mature employees

Direct Energy has more than 2,000 employees, mostly in the Greater Toronto Area. From June 2005 to June 2006, the company recruited almost 100 new 50-plus employees. With fewer younger people interested in the skilled trades, Direct Energy is continuing its efforts to attract mature workers who have the necessary licenses and skills. The company recruits older individuals through a variety of outreach programs including www.matchtheskills.ca, a mature worker website that promotes Direct Energy's progressive work environment, compensation and benefits, and helps build its reputation as a best employer in this category.

Direct Energy found that winning and promoting the *Best Employers Award for 50 Plus Canadians*™ had the additional benefit of increasing its brand awareness among prospective employees in the 50-plus age bracket, who subsequently applied to join the company. The awards have turned out to be a very cost-effective way of recruiting for Direct Energy!

Health benefits

In response to internal survey data, diversity strategy, focus groups and changing demographics, Direct Energy implemented a full and flexible health benefits plan in 2004. Since its inception, employees have been able to tailor their plans to their personal circumstances and choose the right mix of health, dental and other options depending on family or individual needs. The plan allows for several unique standard services, such as the use of a registered massage therapist, without the need for medical consultation, for up to $500 per year.

This flexible benefits plan is a key component of Direct Energy's strategy for retaining mature employees. Some highlights are detailed below.

- In order to align benefits to differing lifestyles, including part-time hours often preferred by semi-retired and retired employees who are returning, full-time benefits are administered after only 20 hours of scheduled work per week and part-time benefits apply for those working more than 14 hours.
- Direct Energy pays health care premiums and provides a $1,400 per year flexible spending account to retired employees (with no age limit).
- There is a short-term disability program that gives all employees financial security in case of illness or injury away from work and allows for up to 120 days of sick pay.
- Employees have the option to receive cash back by reducing coverage to 50% or 80% according to their own lifestyles or waive coverage if covered under another health plan. There are several choices on how to use the extra cash, including the option to increasing savings in the Group Retirement Plan.
- Extra flex-benefit dollars can be used to obtain additional vacation days. This benefits those 50-plus who are interested in working after retirement or plan to reduce work prior to retirement. Unionized Home Services technicians are given an additional two weeks of vacation in their retirement year.
- The use of a drug card and electronic dental payment reduces the financial burden of paying in advance and being reimbursed later. This is an option for mature employees who have other demands on their money such as wealth planning.

- A Flexible Spending Account provides an opportunity to use pre-tax income to pay for health-related expenses not covered under Flex Benefits.
- The Employee Assistance Plan (EAP) keeps mature employees and their family members healthy and productive.

Retirement support

Direct Energy provides several retirement savings vehicles for both long-and short-term employees to maximize their savings for retirement.

- Pension plans: 50-plus employees receive pension contributions from the company with the option of adding personal contributions. Their traditional pension plan mandates that 4% of an employee's salary be contributed by the company.
- Employee share purchase plans: a share purchase program with a company match is available for employees who want to invest in Centrica—Direct Energy's parent company.
- RSP plan and non-registered savings plan: employees are offered a variety of investment options, often with a company-matched contribution of 2.5%. Employees have the opportunity to save through convenient payroll deduction for both the registered savings plan and the non-registered savings plan.
- Workshops and seminars are held throughout the year for those interested in learning more about retirement.

Flexible working arrangements

A number of customized, flexible work situations are available. The company works with the employee to design a plan that meets the needs of the business and the individual. Options include working from home (as many as 60% of Home Services employees work in home settings), compressed and shortened work weeks, and flexible start and finish times.

Flexible working helps retain the valuable skills, knowledge and experience of 50-plus employees.

Vacation and days off

Life-work balance is important to 50-plus employees. Direct Energy workers value the need to relax and rejuvenate in order to be productive at home and in the workplace.

- The Formal Earned Days Off (EDO) program operates in several departments that choose to implement it. It allows for the banking of hours to earn additional time off. For example, an employee that works an additional hour each day can take a half-day off on Friday.
- Unionized employees participate in a more formal program for banked time or earned days off. They also have the choice to sell their banked time back to the company for cash.
- The technical workforce in Home Services can use up to seven floater days. Floater days are simply mutually agreed-upon personal days, which provide employees with a flexible mechanism to balance their commitments at home such as babysitting grandchildren, for example.

Life-long learning

Direct Energy offers life-long learning programs to all employees, including those 50-plus. For example, HVAC technicians are in short supply in many provinces. Direct Energy encourages those employees who may have worked in Direct Energy retail stores selling HVAC parts to become apprentices and have their training and licenses paid for by Direct Energy. Many of those taking advantage of this offer are 50-plus.

The company has developed several initiatives to ensure a culture of life-long learning, including a Tuition Reimbursement Program consisting of 100% sponsorship for external courses that are directly relevant to the job or desired job, and 50% for courses that are indirectly relevant. Others include:

- full reimbursement for professional association dues
- in-house programs such as a comprehensive essentials of management leadership course
- additional bonuses paid for completion of certain accreditation courses are available to all employees
- on-line sales and product knowledge workshops, computer application tutorials and many other self-taught modules
- a unique scholarship program that accepts applications from employees' children for post-secondary education. Eleven students are chosen annually and $1,000 is paid out each year the student is in university or college. This helps 50-plus employees to fund their children's education.

Additionally, the company is continuously upgrading the abilities of its skilled trades employees by offering:

- fully-paid skilled trades licensing upgrading and renewals, with several courses completed during working hours on company property
- a government-approved apprenticeship program that uses direct energy's most experienced tradespeople as trainers
- a mobile training unit that allows employees to learn at remote work locations.

Work environment

Time is taken to assess the work environment; opinions are sought and employee committees are formed. As a result, Direct Energy has comfortable, ergonomic work stations.

- Several locations have onsite gyms and other locations have gyms nearby. employees are given the flexibility to work out at lunch or at other times as mutually agreed. direct energy arranges corporate pricing for these facilities and promotes sports activity.
- Onsite yoga and seated massage is often available and utilized on a fairly regular basis.
- All locations have either a direct energy cafeteria or other local restaurant to ensure a healthy, stable diet.
- Most locations have lounge areas with daily newspapers available; others have quiet rooms that can be used for individual quiet times.
- Main locations have a small library of business and other books of interest that rotate monthly, known as "direct your knowledge space." book clubs have been organized and meet consistently.

Excell Services Ltd.

Address	150 Parkway Place Penticton, BC V2A 8G8
Telephone	250-487-4732
Fax	250-487-4728
Website	www.excellsvcs.com
Type of business	Call centre
Canadian locations	1
Total employees	300
2006, 2007 Award Categories	Recruitment Workplace culture

The company

Excell Services is a call centre that strategically located in the retirement community of Penticton, B.C. The company was interested in attracting an intergenerational workforce, especially a 50-plus cohort, due to the stability, flexibility, interest in part-time work and lack of turnover in this demographic.

Excell Services spends a lot of time asking about the needs of its employees and how to make the workplace better for them. It is rewarded with low turnover rates and an engaged workforce. Excell has developed some interesting training techniques for the 50-plus who have never worked with computers to help them get comfortable with the new technology and help them recruit high-quality employees without those skills, proving that workers who have never worked with computers can learn the skills and be every bit as effective in their jobs as their younger colleagues.

Excell is based in the United States and operates call centres throughout North America, where it is the largest independent provider of directory assistance, operator services and inbound customer service to the telecommunications industry. Replying to requests for residential or business telephone numbers, providing stock quotes, driving directions and weather reports are just a few of the services provided. The company is known for its strong commitment to value and service. The only Canadian centre is in Penticton and has been in operation since July 2001.

Recruitment and retention in a competitive market

Excell is Penticton's largest private employer, operating seven days a week, 24 hours a day. Recruitment is an ongoing process.

Call centres by nature experience high attrition; however, Penticton maintains a lower than average turnover rate. Thirty-five to 40% of the workforce has been with the company since start-up, and 30% of these are 50-plus.

The biggest challenge for Excell is the radically changed labour market in the Penticton region. When Excell opened the Penticton call centre in 2001, a large number of people were seeking employment. By early 2005, recruiting was more difficult and by the end of the year it had reached the point where almost everyone who wanted work was employed. Those few seeking work could pick and choose between many available opportunities in the area. Excell conducted a review of its recruiting policies and procedures in early 2005 and found that what had worked well in the past would not be effective in the future.

Inclusiveness

Excell needed a more innovative approach to compete. Their recruitment initiatives now include widely varied strategies to help find and attract new workers. They may come from often-overlooked communities, including older workers seeking to re-enter the workforce, the physically disabled, First Nations, and people affiliated with the Canadian Armed Forces.

An annual onsite job fair includes a tour of the centre. WorkZone, a government sponsored employment service, has hosted several job fairs on Excell's behalf in the city and surrounding communities. Excell also works closely with On Your Mark Employment, a group helping people return to the workforce after some years.

The company made a concerted effort to draw applicants from the Penticton Indian Band. In November 2005, a job fair was held at the Band's educational facility and Band members were invited to tour the call centre to learn about the job firsthand.

Through a working relationship with Community Futures, Excell was introduced to Achieve BC, an agency that helps the physically disabled find employment. Excell is a good fit with this segment of the workforce as the call centre accommodates those needing a customized workspace. For example, workstation chairs are ergonomically designed and workstations are fully adjustable. There are designated workstations for the hard of hearing, stand-up stations for those unable to sit for lengthy periods of time and stations accessible to wheelchairs. Doors are equipped with easy-entry access buttons. In 2003, Excell received the *Accessible Penticton Award* from the Penticton Chamber of Commerce. In June 2006, Excell was recognized by THEO BC for its involvement, dedication and support of persons with disabilities.

As a member of the Canadian Forces Liaison Council, Excell supports Canadian reservists and has taken steps to ensure that the local squadron is aware the company is hiring.

Setting yourself apart from the competition

Another source of new recruits is the "Refer-A-Friend" program. When an Excell employee successfully refers a friend and the new employee has completed two weeks of training and a full week of call handling, the referring employee has the opportunity to throw darts at balloons to win cash. The opportunity is repeated when the new employee completes 90 and 180 days of employment. The dartboard is located within the work area, where all can watch the fun and be inspired to refer their friends.

Excell keeps job awareness high with another successful initiative—the placement of a large "Now Hiring" banner across the front of the building. The call centre is located near one of the busiest intersections in Penticton and the banner attracts a lot of attention. Many companies in the Penticton region have chosen to spend large amounts of advertising dollars to attract potential employees. With such a depleted labour market, Excell decided not to follow that route and confines its advertising of job opportunities to a series of small classified ads in both local newspapers.

Excell prescreens applicants by testing listening skills, spelling and typing. During the familiarization tour, an applicant may choose to do a trial run through the testing procedure. Individuals leave with the confidence that comes from understanding the testing process should they choose to apply.

Targeting new 50-plus employees

Penticton's temperate climate, coupled with the natural beauty of the Okanagan Valley, makes Penticton a highly desirable retirement area. These demographics made it obvious that Excell needed to reach out to older individuals.

The company quickly realized there was no one way to recruit the 50-plus worker because the interests, skills and work experience of this demographic are so diverse. Excell determined that word of mouth and personal referrals were the best options for reaching this segment of the labour force.

Within the past 12 months, 47 mature workers have been hired. Excell offers employment opportunities that allow the 50-plus worker to continue developing skills and abilities. The company recognizes that older employees have a good work ethic and provide positive role models for other staff. As a result, Excell goes to great lengths to assure those 50-plus that they are welcome and very much appreciated.

Community relations

Excell desires to be recognized as the "employer of choice" in the Penticton area, a designation that would obviously benefit both recruiting and retention—especially of those 50-plus. To do so meant increasing community awareness, industry understanding and personal referrals. As a result, Excell decided to employ a full-time Community Relations Manager.

The Community Relations Manager works with businesses and individuals in the region, providing information about employment opportunities with Excell. Despite the fact that call centres are the fastest-growing industry in Canada, there are still many who do not understand the nature of the business. Excell was the first call centre to open in the region, and the CRM takes every opportunity to address community groups to increase general knowledge of the industry.

Further enhancing community awareness is Excell's employee-based Community Involvement Committee. The CIC supports a broad range of philanthropic activities including arts, education, minor sports and local charitable foundations. In 2004, Excell was awarded the Corporate Citizen Award by the Penticton Chamber of Commerce.

Flexo Products

Address	4777 Kent Avenue Niagara Falls, ON L2H 1J5
Telephone	905-354-2723
Fax	905-354-1301
Website	www.flexoproducts.com
Type of business	Cleaning supplies and equipment manufacturer and supplier
Canadian locations	3
Total employees	65
2006, 2007 Award categories	Recruitment Retention Health Management practices Retirement/retiree practices

The company

Since 1918, Flexo Products has supplied consumers with a wide array of cleaning products that today range from cleaning chemicals to floor finishes, recycling systems to maintenance equipment and paper supplies. These products are constantly scrutinized and upgraded to take advantage of new technologies. The company prides itself on providing unparalleled service, quality and value to clients. It utilizes a fleet of vehicles to ensure prompt delivery and trained personnel to provide quick answers on product choice and delivery.

Flexo Products is a privately held company headquartered in Niagara Falls, Ontario with offices in Toronto and Cambridge, and employ 65 employees, with approximately 40% 50-plus. One member of the administrative staff is older than 70.

Flexo Products found dramatic changes in company safety and morale when they began introducing 50-plus workers into the workplace. It was an eye-opening experience for management and led to acceptance of and an increasing reliance on the 50-plus demographic in its workforce.

For example, Flexo introduced a free chiropractic assessment for their manufacturing employees. Many male employees took advantage of the onsite service to find out how to strengthen and support muscles that were vulnerable to injury due to the stress and strain of their jobs. This one service helped Flexo save thousands of dollars of benefits costs when employees found a way to be proactive with muscle strains rather than taking time off to "rest" their bodies.

Recruitment: all it takes is one

Several years ago, Flexo hired an older worker in its plant. The arrangement worked out so well that it led Flexo to rethink its general practice of hiring younger people subsidized by the government to work at Flexo. The company had experienced a constant turnover among its younger workers and absenteeism was high. More alarming was a high accident rate in the factory. The company realized the value of older workers and began actively recruiting mature people. As the mean age of the workforce increased, Flexo's turnover, absenteeism and accident rates went down.

The company also increased its efforts to retain existing long-term staff. For example, a 65-year-old Flexo Products employee announced his decision to retire two years ago, but Flexo was reluctant to lose his skills and experience. So munagement asked the employee to consider working a reduced work week. The employee agreed and today is still working a three-day-a-week schedule.

Flexo Products has also benefited from downsizings in the manufacturing sector. It saw that a pool of relatively young, physically capable individuals existed, individuals who had been laid off from manufacturing jobs and were seeking new employment. Flexo could not offer the substantial incomes many of these individuals were used to, but management made it clear that this was an organization that welcomed 50-plus workers.

Over the past few years, the attitude of Flexo supervisors towards older workers has changed radically. Replacing wariness is a "welcome aboard, let's see what you can do" philosophy. That's because older workers have brought stability to the organization.

Chiropractic adjustments for healthier workers and bottom line

Many Flexo employees are involved in physical work, with strains and musculoskeletal issues a frequent occurence. Flexo found that when it referred employees to their family physicians, rest and medication were often the recommended course of action. Flexo thought a more proactive approach was needed and arranged for a chiropractor to visit the facility once a week, with the company picking up the tab for an employee's first consultation. Since introducing this initiative two years ago, Flexo Products has greatly reduced its short-term disability costs related to musculoskeletal issues and employee feedback has been extremely positive. Employees report getting relief from long-term strains and enjoying a better quality of life as a result of the chiropractic care. Indeed, many have admitted they would never have thought of seeking chiropractic services if Flexo Products had not introduced the program. New employees are now routinely assessed by the company chiropractor to determine if any part of their bodies needs strengthening in order to prevent future injury.

Flexo Products also invested considerable time training the chiropractor on the various jobs within the organization so the chiropractor could also serve as company's ergonomic specialist. This in-house chiropractic and ergonomic expertise had an additional, unexpected value when the company recently relocated. This program has more than paid for itself in reduced short-term disability and by improving the quality of life for Flexo employees.

The Home Depot Canada Inc.

Address	900–1 Concorde Gate Toronto, ON M3C 4H9
Telephone	416-609-0852
Fax	416-412-4958
Website	www.homedepot.ca
Type of business	Home improvement retailer
Canadian locations	155
Total employees	27,000+ (Canada)
2005 Award categories	Recruitment Retention Career development Workplace culture

The company

The Home Depot is a pioneer retailer, one of the first companies to recognize the absolute strategic value of bringing experienced and loyal 50-plus workers into the workforce. Approximately 20% of its current workforce is 50-plus and the number is growing. With a commitment to ensuring that its associate base reflects the communities served, Home Depot will increase the proportion of 50-plus sales associates as that segment of the population explodes.

The Home Depot focuses on employee development on the job and is one of the few organizations where training is ongoing, with performance reviews twice a year to help people stay on a career path of ever-expanding knowledge. The company embraces the skills and experience that mature prospects bring to its retail stores, actively seeking the 50-plus employee for that reason.

The world's largest home improvement retailer, The Home Depot caters to do-it-yourselfers and home improvement, construction and building maintenance professionals. Each store stocks approximately 40,000 to 50,000 different kinds of building materials, home improvement supplies and lawn and garden products. It currently operates in seven Canadian provinces (Alberta, British Columbia, Manitoba, Nova Scotia, Ontario, Quebec and Saskatchewan), 49 U.S. states, Puerto Rico and Mexico. There are more than 27,000 employees in Canada.

Home Depot stock is publicly traded (NYSE:HD) and is included in the Standard & Poor's 500 Index and the Dow Jones 30 Industrial Index. For eight consecutive years, The Home Depot has been ranked by *Fortune* magazine as America's Most Admired Specialty Retailer.

The 50-plus advantage

In terms of 50-plus employment, The Home Depot is noted for:
- their early recognition of the strategic value of hiring 50-plus associates
- the fact that 20% of their current workforce is 50-plus
- continued training and development for all associates
- second career/leadership opportunities
- outreach to increase awareness of job opportunities and reach out to the 50-plus demographic.

Store managers and Human Resources managers at The Home Depot Canada have the responsibility to hire the best talent possible to meet the needs of customers and to drive sales. It has long been recognized at Home Depot that the 50-plus population can do both exceptionally well. This demographic represents almost 20% of the company's workforce, a number that is expected to explode as the baby boomers continue to age and Home Depot continues to grow.

Given that almost 50% of our population will be 50-plus by the year 2015, The Home Depot considers it good business sense to attract associates from this group.

The Home Depot Canada's hiring needs are ongoing as the company opens new stores in communities across the country, with growth expected to continue at a rapid pace in the years ahead. Each store in Canada is responsible for building a hiring plan that meets the unique requirements for that store, a plan that takes into account a good full-and part-time mix, seasonal hiring adjustments, turnover trends, and the technical expertise required to meet customer needs in key departments. Each store looks to the 50-plus population within the community to meet these needs.

The Home Depot provides training in order to increase its associates' knowledge base about their department but doesn't stop there. When training is completed associates are asked if they would like to learn about adjacent departments. The 50-plus workforce sets the bar high in this area. Their maturity, availability, knowledge and courteous, friendly manner are all key reasons why Home Depot works hard to attract, motivate and retain its 50-plus sales associates. Performance reviews are ongoing with a formal review twice a year, for employees and the company to ensure that learning is an integral part of the job process.

"Ability is ageless..."

According to corporate research, there are five main reasons that 50-plus workers seek employment at the Home Depot:
- to supplement retirement income
- flexible work schedules
- social interaction with fellow associates and customers
- ongoing training and development
- an opportunity for a second career.

"I couldn't stand retirement," says one mature Home Depot associate. "There were too many hours in the day to do nothing. I enjoy working and helping the company to reach its goals."

Finding a second career can be a daunting task for mature workers. But once hired in sales, many of The Home Depot's 50-plus associates quickly demonstrate their leadership skills and find themselves in supervisory or management positions within the stores. When asked, many mentioned that The Home Depot was like a "second chance" and noted that that their wish to continue to develop and learn new things was fulfilled at The Home Depot Canada. "I need to work," said one 50-plus associate. "My ability is ageless, which is why I chose The Home Depot."

A corporate culture of community service

The Home Depot not only reflects the community it serves in its workforce hiring composition, but also believes in giving back. Team Depot, an organized volunteer force, was developed in 1992 to allow associates to contribute to the communities where they work and live. The Home Depot Canada has been recognized at the Retail Council of Canada's Excellence in Retailing Awards, receiving the Community Outreach Award for making a significant contribution to the community.

Innovation in recruitment

The Home Depot looks to the future with these distinct corporate goals:

- capitalizing on the perception of The Home Depot canada as being "a great place to work"
- targeted recruiting efforts
- on-line job postings at www.theskillsmatch.ca
- continually reviewing employment practices.

The Home Depot's strategic focus on hiring takes many of the recommendations made by their 50-plus associates into consideration. When asked what Home Depot could do to attract more associates from the 50-plus demographic, workers said the company could do a better job with targeted advertising. Associates have also made recommendations regarding benefits enhancements, more opportunities for personal leave without pay and more fixed shifts.

Home Instead Senior Care

Address	1210 Sheppard Avenue East, Suite 4 Toronto, ON M2K 1E3
Telephone	416-512-8989
Fax	416-512-0052
Website	www.homeinstead.com
Type of business	Homemaking agency
Canadian locations	16
Total employees	600+
2006 Award Categories	Recruitment Retention Career development Management practices

The company

Home Instead Senior Care prides itself on the training and support it provides its caregivers, 76% of whom are 50-plus. These caregivers are encouraged to use their life experience to help those who need basic homemaking and housekeeping to stay in their homes. Home Instead surveys its caregivers annually to look for ways to improve working conditions and its support of the workforce, which is very unusual in this line of work. Home Instead Senior Care has also developed a unique training program for caregivers.

Home Instead Senior Care is the world's largest provider of comprehensive companionship and homecare services for seniors. These services are provided through a network of franchise offices located throughout the U.S., Canada, Japan, Portugal, Australia, Ireland, New Zealand and the U.K.

Leaving familiar surroundings and the comfort and security of home isn't always necessary for many older adults. Home Instead caregivers help seniors live independently, no matter where they call home. For anywhere from a few hours a day up to around-the-clock-care, seven days a week and holidays, thousands of older adults receive help with everyday tasks like meal preparation, reminders to take medication, laundry, light housekeeping, shopping and errands.

The company has provided care to nearly one million clients since its founding in 1994 in Omaha, Nebraska.

Mature workers

Home Instead Senior Care's mission is to be "the world's trusted nonmedical source of companionship and home care for the elderly." Achievement of this goal begins with the individual caregiver, and must only be accomplished one relationship at a time. Home Instead Senior Care strives to hire only the most trustworthy and passionate individuals as caregivers. Clients and their loved ones can be assured that caregivers know how to respond to unique situations and have learned techniques to manage the challenges of the aging process.

Home Instead Senior Care realizes that the 50-plus worker brings invaluable experience, patience and commitment to eldercare work. Home Instead caregivers are hired from all walks of life and may be highly educated professionals or retired homemakers. Their life skills and experiences bring joy daily to the lives of seniors. Today, more than 76% of Canadian Home Instead caregivers are 50-plus and many are more than 75 years old. Mature caregivers often have common interests with their clients and together they can share memories of a particular era. Great effort is made to match caregivers to clients so that everyone involved grows and benefits from the relationship.

Career development through training

What sets Home Instead Senior Care apart from other nonmedical eldercare companies is their dedication to training and education.

Special training and recognition programs have been developed to enhance the skills of caregivers and to honour their compassion for older adults. Creating accessible materials that address the serious job of caring for seniors was a challenge, because caregivers come from all different walks of life, with different education levels, ages and economic classes. The training program encompasses five phases:

- GRAD I (Growth Through Reading and Development)
- Safety Training Guide
- GRAD II
- Caregiver Activity Training Guide
- Alzheimer Caregiver Training Program.

Recognition

Older workers become caregivers because they want to be useful, productive and contribute to their communities. Home Instead Senior Care's annual survey proves this year after year, and the company has developed a number of ways to recognize and honour this.

All local offices have a Caregiver of the Month program. These individuals are honoured at one of the regular caregiver meetings with a recognition pin and gifts. Each monthly honouree is then considered for Caregiver of the Year in their community. As there are over 500 offices in North America, the area is divided into seven regions. The Home Office awards a Regional Caregiver Award, and finally the Caregiver of the Year Award is presented at the Annual Convention at a gala event. The winning caregiver receives a trip to the convention and is Home Instead Senior Care's honoured guest. The winning caregiver's portrait is displayed in the Home Office with the previous years' winners. The caregiver is also honoured on the Home Instead Senior Care website and in *Seniorcare Connections*, the company's quarterly newsletter.

Recruitment by 50-plus peers

Caregivers are the best source of recruitment for other caregivers. Caregivers are rewarded with $25 for each referral, but the biggest reward for them is that they get to work with friends and family.

Retention

Home Instead caregivers have flexible hours, working as little or as much as they choose. This is important to mature workers as they want to be in control of their time. Home Instead Senior Care office staff work closely with caregivers to develop work schedules that suit their lifestyles and meets the needs of their clients.

Merck Frosst Canada Ltd.

Address	16711 TransCanada Highway Kirkland, PQ H9H 3L1
Telephone	514-428-7920
Fax	514-428-4906
Website	www.merckfrosst.com
Type of business	Pharmaceutical
Canadian locations	9
Total employees	1600
2005, 2006, 2007 Award categories	Retention Career development Management practices Retirement/retiree practices Benefits

The company

An annual winner since the inception of The *Best Employers Award for 50 Plus Canadians™*, Merck Frosst continues to improve the support available to its 50-plus workers every year. Recently, the company added new insurance products for their employees and continues to refine its mentoring program.

Merck Frosst, headquartered in Montreal, is one of Canada's leading research-based pharmaceutical companies and has a long record of innovation. The company employs 1,600 people, including more than 300 of the world's leading scientific personnel. The Merck Frosst Centre for Therapeutic Research, one of the largest biomedical research facilities in Canada, has a mandate to discover new therapies for the treatment of respiratory diseases, inflammatory diseases, hypertension, diabetes and osteoporosis.

Merck Frosst markets an extensive line of cardiovascular products for high blood pressure, elevated cholesterol and heart failure as well as a broad range of vaccines. The company is a recognized leader in the treatment of asthma, osteoporosis, HIV/AIDS, glaucoma, prostate disease, migraines and infectious diseases.

The company is firmly committed to science education and sponsors a number of programs across the country designed to spark young people's interest in science.

Employee feedback

Merck Frosst continually listens to its employees, and many needs, including those of its 50-plus staff, are identified in feedback received through employee surveys,

Merck Frosst has had an Employee Advisory Council for several years so that the views, opinions, and suggestions of employees are communicated and represented to management. The EAC actively provides input into the creation and revision of company and human resources policies, practices, procedures, and programs.

Employees can also submit questions to senior management via a confidential e-mail address set up for this purpose. Responses are included in the weekly employee newsletter.

Training and development

Merck Frosst encourages continual learning throughout an employee's career regardless of age. The company has established. a variety of programs that allow employees to choose their preferred way to learn and what resources best suit their learning style.

Every year, employees have the opportunity to formally review their developmental objectives and career goals with their manager. One tool used to facilitate this process is the Employee Developments Plan. This tool allows employees and their managers to build a plan that supports the development of individual competencies and helps people reach their fullest potential within their current and future jobs.

Promotion

Merck Frosst encourages promotion based on performance and experience, not on age. They have 50-plus employees at all levels of the organization including Manager, Director and Vice President. These individuals achieved this measure of success based on their experience and performance.

"I began my career at Merck Frosst when I was already in my 50s. When I was so well received, by my mostly much younger colleagues, I knew that I had made the right decision to join the company," says Sheila Murphy, Manager of Public Affairs. "And the best news is I am having a great time! My job at Merck Frosst offers me stimulating professional challenges with opportunities to learn every day."

Retaining and recognizing mature employees

Of Merck Frosst's 1,600 employees, almost 300 are over 50. Of those, 62 are in managerial roles.

Talent retention is one of Merck Frosst's key objectives. Towards that end, the company has taken significant steps to encourage knowledge transfer through the use of formal and informal mentoring programs. The formal mentoring program is a voluntary, 12-month program that encourages two-way learning and fosters cross-functional knowledge. The result is an ongoing sharing of experiences. Many mentors are 50-plus.

To recognize long-term and retiring employees, a 25-Year Banquet is a yearly event which offers cocktails, dinner, entertainment and dancing to thank these employees for their dedication and loyalty to the company.

Innovative benefits

Merck Frosst has created a flexible benefits program that can be adapted to the changing needs of its employees, specifically those who at 50-plus encounter changing family circumstances such as dependent or spousal support.

One such initiative is the SavingsPlus Account. This is separate from RRSPs and offers Merck employees the added advantage of further tax deductions while helping them save toward their retirement. Almost one quarter of contributors are 50-plus employees.

Merck Frosst believes that a productive work environment is one that respects employees and their differences, fosters teamwork, promotes flexibility and supports a healthy balance between an employee's work and personal life. Flexible work arrangements are part of this philosophy and are popular with employees of all ages, but especially with older employees caring for elderly parents.

In 2004, Merck Frosst launched its Planned Personal Leave program, an unpaid leave of absence planned in collaboration with and the approval of management. This is a discretionary privilege, granted on the basis of specific criteria such as seniority and performance. This program differs from other temporary leave programs, such as maternity, parental, disability and bereavement leaves, in one significant way. Employees don't have to wait until retirement to take a break and make their dreams come true, they can use the Personal Leave Program as a trial retirement. The company provides a three-hour financial counseling session to help employees take advantage of all the benefits this program offers. During the leave, employees' seniority continues to accumulate, as do their pension credits and all Group Insurance Benefits. In addition, a similar position to the one left is guaranteed upon the employee's return.

The Planned Personal Leave program allows employees to achieve the right balance between their personal needs and those of the organization.

Keeping up with retirees

What sets Merck Frosst apart from many other organizations is its efforts to retain close ties with retired employees.

In 1999, a Merck Frosst Retiree Committee was created to represent the interests of current and future retirees and to bring issues of concern to MF management. The committee meets quarterly and is composed of retiree representatives and an appointed employer representative. The Retiree Luncheon, the Retiree's Directory and the Retiree Survey were all initiatives of this Committee.

A yearly luncheon is organized to provide an opportunity for former employees to meet and keep in touch with friends and colleagues.

In 1999, a Retiree Directory was initiated to enable Merck Frosst retirees to communicate with each other. Retirees whose names are published give their permission to include relevant information and are informed of such a publication upon their retirement.

A 20-page brochure describing retiree benefits is given to all retiring employees. The booklet provides an overview of insurance coverage and information about coverage under various other Merck Frosst programs. Also included is a "Who to Call List" outlining important contact information regarding pension and insurance providers.

The Merck Frosst Retiree Hotline is a toll-free hotline that provides retirees with accurate information within one business day. An Employee Services agent is always available during business hours.

Merck Frosst provides an excellent retirement plan and the right tools to help its employees prepare for their financial independence. Information seminars are conducted to help them understand these and other benefit programs.

Metasoft Systems Inc.

Address	203–1080 Howe Street Vancouver, BC V6Z 2T1
Telephone	604-683-6711
Fax	604-683-6704
Website	www.bigdatabase.com/careers
Type of business	Software development; fundraising systems
Canadian locations	3
Total employees	90
2007 Award categories	Recruitment Retention Career development Workplace culture

The company

Metasoft Systems operates a very interesting business, providing support to nonprofit organizations on how to access funds from various foundations around the world. It often hires people with little or no experience with computers, but plenty of passion for a particular charitable cause or endeavour, such as women's shelters or children with disabilities. Some of its most successful employees are 50-plus. Their ability to communicate that passion all day long helps them connect with Metasoft's clients who share the same mission, and helps them succeed in their work. In addition to its 50-plus employee cohort, another HR fact about Metasoft that sets it apart from other high-tech, IT companies is that more than half of their managers are women.

Metasoft operates two distinct and highly successful business units: a software development division offering a suite of software components for messaging, document management, conversion and imaging, and a fundraising division providing an online, searchable database of corporate, foundation and government grant-making information to thousands of nonprofits worldwide. Founded in 1988, Metasoft is now North America's leading source of funding information and services for the nonprofit sector.

Headquartered in Vancouver, B.C., Metasoft has offices in Halifax, Nova Scotia and St. John's, Newfoundland. It is a Branham/Financial Post Top 300 Canadian Technology Company and donates 5% of its pre-tax profits in the form of money, time and other resources to further good causes.

Recruiting

Metasoft's recruiting mission is to hire great people who want to increase their earning and career potential while helping nonprofit organizations realize their philanthropic goals. In the words of Metasoft's recruiting manager, Cathy Lim, the perfect candidate is "a highly motivated and goal-driven individual with excellent communication and analytical skills, and a track record of proven sales success...and mature."

As Metasoft begins to enter the global market, especially the U.K. , they find they cannot attract talent fast enough to meet their clients' needs.

Mature employees fit the company and the client

The demographics at Metasoft are extremely unusual for a software company. First, 70% of their staff is female and second, the average age is around 40, with sales staff averaging 45. Generally, those employed in this sector tend to be young males, especially in management positions.

Metasoft has found that mature people stay with the company longer, care about their clients and develop relationships that allow them to become very successful salespeople. (More than half of the staff is in sales.)

In order to understand Metasoft's commitment to the recruitment and retention of mature workers, one has to first understand their customers. The average age of an employee in the nonprofit sector in Canada is over 50 and the majority of them rank their company's mission as more important than their pay cheque. Many have left successful careers in the for-profit sector to work for a cause they believe makes a difference in the world. So it's not surprising that Metasoft customers appreciate the same high level of engagement and maturity from Metasoft employees. Incidentally, 25% of Metasoft employees are involved in charity work outside of their workplace.

The company has every intention of not only adding to its mature workforce through new hires, but by encouraging employee longevity with them. Metasoft's current retention rate of 92% for its 50-plus employees suggests they are on the right track.

Hi-tech friendly

Metasoft realizes there are some unique challenges facing a 50-plus worker considering a career change. Retraining, particularly in the information technology field, can be particularly intimidating. Fortunately, although Metasoft's product is considered cutting-edge in the technology world, it doesn't take cutting-edge technology skills to use or sell it. In fact, a new hire may require only basic IT skills training, which Metasoft is happy to provide. Metasoft considers this a good investment. Two of their top sales representatives, both 50-plus, did not even know how to turn on a computer when they began with the company!

There is little doubt that Metasoft is acting in its own interest in recruiting and retaining the mature worker. It knows that 50-plus workers add more value to the business than any other demographic. It has found older individuals bring a commitment and a passion to their work that is hard to find elsewhere. "For those reasons, we will continue to celebrate our mature workers, and we will do our best to ensure that their career with us is both successful and fulfilling," says Cathy Lim.

"What makes Metasoft one of the best employers transcends generations," says Cathy Lim. "There are many companies [that] turn a good profit, and many that make a difference in the world, but there are few that do both. We get to come to work every day knowing that what we do is not only making the world a better place, but [that we] are creating a business success story. It doesn't get more rewarding than this, no matter what age you are."

Support, recruitment and retention

Metasoft has introduced several initiatives to not only support its existing mature workforce, but to attract and retain new talent from the 50-plus demographic. In 2003, Metasoft introduced a work-from-home initiative that has been a great success. Currently, 18% of Metasoft's staff work from home full-time, and 6% part-time. Metasoft has found that for mature employees, the amount of time saved by not commuting and the ability to work flexible hours equates to more quality time with family and for other interests and hobbies. In addition, employees may apply for an unpaid leave of absence at any time, allowing for extra vacations—a provision appreciated by the mature worker who has a retired partner, for example.

The company's social calendar ensures that there are plenty of opportunities for employees and their families to get to know one another. Summer softball, barbeques, family movies, trips and pitch-and-putt tournaments are just some of the fully subsidized activities offered. In addition, the company's book club appeals to older employees.

Metasoft also likes to recognize and reward long-serving employees. Each annual milestone of employment is acknowledged with a company-wide e-mail and a gift. After one year of employment, employees receive a down vest; after five, a trip to Vegas; and after 10, an Alaskan cruise.

Employee surveys are regularly conducted to discern job satisfaction, job engagement and health and wellness needs. Metasoft acts on the findings of all surveys.

Growth and opportunity

Metasoft makes personal growth opportunities a priority for its employees, preferring to promote from within. Entry-level positions are recognized as springboards to further opportunities.

A flexible and creative workplace culture

Metasoft promotes a flexible atmosphere with a casual dress code and an ideal blend of employee spirit and autonomy to keep employees energized and working creatively.

The company is committed to employee equity and diversity, employing an array of high-achievement-oriented people from different cultures and backgrounds. Metasoft believes that diversity is a key to its continuing success and as the company grows, it is expanding its search for talent around the world.

Benefits

Metasoft's customized benefits plan reflects the changing needs of its employees. The company offers a highly competitive compensation package as well as health and wellness initiatives. "We ensure that our employees' needs are met by encouraging a healthy work-life balance, and taking an active role in our community," says Cathy Lim.

Metasoft offers:
- An onsite gym, in the Vancouver location
- Onsite monthly chair massage
- Employee and family assistance program
- Awards and recognition program
- Employee recruiting referral program.

Orkin PCO Services Corporation

Address	5840 Falbourne Street Mississauga, ON L5R 4B5
Telephone	905-502-9700
Fax	905-502-9511
Website	www.pco.com
Type of business	Pest Control
Canadian locations	Across Canada
Total employees	548
2006 Award category	Retirement /retiree practices

The company

Orkin PCO Services could see trouble on the horizon. Industry training programs were not producing enough new workers to meet demand. Meanwhile, many 50-plus employees were finding full-time work too demanding, but were not ready or eligible for retirement and its subsequent loss of benefits. The award-winning solution for the company and its employees? Orkin designed a more flexible work schedule that included part-time options for its valued mature workers, letting them choose the workload they wanted without losing benefits. And when 50-plus employees were given the opportunity to move into training and mentoring roles within the company, everyone won. Orkin retained both the services and the institutional knowledge of its most experienced workers in a very competitive labour market.

Orkin PCO is Canada's largest and most respected pest control company, with locations from coast to coast. The company is constantly developing more effective and environmentally responsible pest control products and application techniques. Orkin PCO has set the Canadian standard in technology for pest management and prevention in all categories of business—whether residential, manufacturing, commercial, industrial, shipping, mining, grain or government.

Orkin PCO collaborates with industry on future management techniques to monitor and safeguard people and livestock from such diseases as the West Nile virus and hantavirus. Their research continues daily with nine full-time entomologists.

Although well trained and licensed to handle and apply pest control materials Orkin PCO is also aggressively seeking green or organic solutions to the pest problems.

The regular part-time option for 50-plus workers

Researchers may develop new methods of pest control, but for customers, pest control is in the hands of the technicians. These technicians are qualified and accredited Integrated Pest Management (IPM) specialists who adhere to strict government regulations, including provincial licensing, and who are continuously challenged with rigorous examinations.

In Ontario, Orkin was facing a unique dilemma. The only school to offer training in pest control had closed the program. And as technicians retired, Orkin had no easy access to or source of new, trained technicians.

The solution was two-fold. First, persuade older technicians to remain on the job and second, provide training and mentoring programs for interested young people. Orkin did this by a creating a new category of work within the organization: regular part-time.

Regular part-time positions are for mature employees who have not yet reached the age of full retirement but would like to cut back their work week and still enjoy the benefits of being part of the organization. Technicians wishing to continue working past the traditional retirement age of 65 can also take advantage of this initiative.

Regular part-time employees are hired for an indefinite period but with part-time hours of 20 to 39 hours per week. The employee retains all the benefits, advantages and access to programs of a full-time employee, including dental, health, vision, life insurance, short-term disability and long-term disability benefits.

The program has proved a great success for all involved. Older employees enjoy greater flexibility and an opportunity to ease into retirement, or to remain working as long as they are able to perform their job duties. Younger workers have an irreplaceable source of knowledge and Orkin retains valuable skills and experience.

The real beneficiary, however, is the public. Safe, effective pest control is not only a business issue—it is a health issue, and access to trained personnel who can control the pest population is vital now and in the future.

Training and development

For Orkin employees of all ages, the training never ends. There is both on-the-job training and branch manager training. In addition, employees from all districts attend regular seminars dealing with new developments in pest control and management such as simpler and safer new applications techniques, safety measures and environmental concerns.

RBC Global Banking Service Centre

Address	20 King Street West Toronto, ON M5H 1C4
Telephone	416-974-1964
Fax	416-974-1444
Website	www.rbc.com
Type of business	Banking
Canadian locations	4
Total employees	150+
2005 Award categories	Recruitment Retention Career development Workplace culture Management practices Retirement/retiree practices Diversity in the workplace

The company

RBC Global Banking Service Centre was determined not to lose the intellectual capital that specific employees had built up over many years of service with a bank. The company cherry-picked these employees from other divisions of RBC and recruited them for a highly specialized unit that deals with complex contracts around the world.

The Global Banking Service Centre (GBSC) is part of RBC—Global Technology & Operations Platform in Royal Bank Group of Companies. GBSC services Royal Bank's top-tier corporate, national government, institutional, broker dealer and nonbank financial institutions with complex and global operations requiring demanding financial expertise. Customer relationships originate in Canada, the United States, Latin America, Europe and Asia Pacific.

The majority of GBSC staff are based in Toronto, but there are offices in Montreal, Calgary and Vancouver.

Mature employees are a return on investment

The Global Banking Service Centre provides RBC's top-tier corporate clients with domestic and global loans administration and cash management servicing. The nature of the business requires people with top-level business and behavioural skills, experience and dedication. The Centre tries to attract and retain people with extensive experience in financial services and business in general, as well as the know-how to manage the intricacies of dealing with major multinational accounts. At GBSC, maturity is a valued asset.

For RBC's Global Banking Services Centre, older workers represent a return on investment. Over the course of an employee's banking career, RBC commits a great deal towards training, developing and honing the worker's financial and business skills. By the time retirement looms, that employee has usually risen in the ranks and has considerable responsibility and knowledge. Retirement means a loss for the organization in expertise, experience and education, not to mention the time and expense to train and nurture a replacement.

Seeing an opportunity to retain that wealth of knowledge and maturity, GBSC has begun to recruit employees with specific skills who are about to retire from other areas of the bank. Once retired, the employee is hired back on a contract basis by GBSC.

GSBC happily accommodates retirees by allowing flexible working arrangements. Some work a few hours a day, some two or three days a week and some full-time for short-term assignments. One staff member works only during the summer months. Winter finds him enjoying the Caribbean sun.

Many of these "recruits" are well beyond the age of traditional retirement.

It's not only the extra income that lures these seasoned professionals back to RBC. Most say they missed the social interaction of working as well as the chance of continuing to contribute years of financial and business experience to the operation of Canada's leading financial institution.

"These individuals aren't sitting at home twiddling their thumbs," says David Sullivan, centre manager for GBSC. "They're active in their communities, pursuing their interests, travelling and enjoying their retirement. They're busy people."

Seven Oaks General Hospital

Address	2300 Mc Phillips Street Winnipeg, MN R2V 3M3
Telephone	(204) 632-7133
Fax	(204) 694-9469
Website	www.sogh.mb.ca
Type of business	Health care
Canadian locations	1
Total employees	1400
2006, 2007 Award categories	Recruitment retention Workplace culture Management practices

The organization

Seven Oaks General Hospital (SOGH) is the key provider of health care to residents of the entire Winnipeg region, as well as the Selkirk, Stonewall and Interlake areas. Established in 1981, Seven Oaks is an accredited, 275-bed acute-care facility offering a wide range of services including medical, surgical, ambulatory, rehabilitation, geriatric, emergency, mental health services, renal health and health promotion and disease prevention services.

What is so remarkable and award-worthy about this organization? It's the way Seven Oaks continuously promotes and supports the health of its own employees, not just the patients it serves. Never content to rest on its laurels, SOGH strives to improve on an already outstanding record of reduced injuries and retention of health care staff.

Over the last 20 years, the hospital has initiated many innovative approaches to health care, such as Program Management, Patient Caremap system, Bed Management practices and the Wellness Institute.

Seven Oaks has received the Human Resource Leadership award from the Human Resources Management Association of Manitoba and a Top 100 Employer Award (2005 & 2006) from *MacLean's Magazine*.

Baby boomer nurses

SOGH is fairly typical of healthcare employers in that half of its staff is 45 or older. That percentage is rising, due to the high representation of baby boomers who began their career in health care in the 1970s and now occupy key positions in many organizations.

Like elsewhere in Canada, one in three nurses are 50-plus, and nurses are the largest occupational group at SOGH. Given the intense focus on improving Canada's health care system, hospitals across the country have been under great pressure to recruit and retain nurses, whose demanding occupations put them at high risk for injury, stress and burnout. The nursing situation is also complicated by the fact that Canada is not graduating enough nurses to replace the ones who are eligible to retire early or who are leaving the profession altogether.

Retention

Seven Oaks implemented a comprehensive Healthy Organization Strategy in 2001 that formed the basis for its plan to retain and support older workers, especially nurses. This strategy doesn't exclude younger workers, but its primary focus is employees who are beginning to experience elevated risks of chronic disease, chronic injury, and work-life balance issues. The purpose of the Health Organization Strategy is "to encourage optimal health for all SOGH employees while cultivating a positive healthy culture where employees choose to work, thus laying the foundation for exceptional productivity, extraordinary clinical excellence and outstanding patient satisfaction."

Developing a healthy corporate culture

Prior to launching the new strategy, SOGH reviewed and revised its mission, vision and values. New core values were developed to define the desired organizational culture—one that focuses on people. The new core values are: integrity, person-centred, quality, learning, wellness, team, spirituality and stewardship.

Improving the health and fitness of employees

To promote healthy lifestyle behaviours and to prevent illness, injury and disability, SOGH offers an award-winning workplace wellness program. SOGH provides funding for a full-time coordinator to facilitate the program as well as funding for program interventions. The Seven Oaks model consists of seven steps.

1. Capturing senior level support

Management has been educated about the link between employee health, productivity and cost management.

2. Creating cohesive wellness teams

Each program/service department has its own workplace wellness team consisting of 8–15 employees representing a variety of occupations and levels to develop, guide and oversee the area's wellness efforts.

3. Identifying employee health risks

Every employee is entitled to a free Health Risk Appraisal (HRA) that provides a confidential, individualized report on his or her health risks and corresponding recommendations on what can be done to reduce those risks. The data collected in the HRA drives the operating plans, behaviour change goals and disease management efforts.

4. Crafting an operating plan

Each program/service area has an annual operating plan that articulates the strategic direction including the specific goals and objectives, budget, communication plan, progress and evaluation plan.

5. Choosing appropriate interventions

Interventions depend on the risk factors prevalent in the employee population, what interests the employees and the amount of resources available in a given year.

Examples of previous interventions include:
- risk reduction programs like weight management and smoking cessation
- body-mind exercise programs
- walking and running clubs
- nutritional counselling
- onsite massage and reflexology
- regular health screenings for cholesterol, blood pressure and blood sugars
- stress management programs
- health education classes.

In addition to these targeted interventions, SOGH provides a discounted membership and the first three months free at the Wellness Institute (WI)—an onsite, state-of-the-art, 80,000 square foot medical fitness facility.

6. Creating a supportive environment

Some of the many features that make SOGH a supportive environment are:

- Vending machines with healthy food choices
- Healthy Café-full service
- The Wellness Institute
- Walking paths—the outdoor track/park area at the WI
- Outdoor meditation courtyard
- No smoking facility and grounds
- Work stations conform to ergonomic standards
- Safety hazards have been eliminated
- Lockers and showers are available for employees.

7. Consistently evaluating outcomes

SOGH measures the workplace wellness program effectiveness using indicators such as participation levels, and absenteeism and retention rates.

Occupational safety and health programs

SOGH also has several established programs and services to help employees with short acute or long-term injuries, illnesses and conditions. Employees are able to access the following:

- critical incident stress management counselling—24/7 consultation
- workplace safety and health committee
- disability management program
- injured workers program: a free onsite musculoskeletal intervention program gives employees access to occupational therapists, physiotherapists, chiropractor, and family physician
- employee health nurse-access to an onsite occupational health nurse for treatment and/or referral

- Employee Assistance Program—a confidential service that provides professional assessment, referral, and access to counselling services to help employers and family members with family or marital concerns, workplace problems, drug or alcohol abuse, and stress, depression or emotional problems
- grief ministry
- injury prevention training.

Work-life balance initiatives

SOGH offers employees a number of work-life programs and services, among them:
- reduction of work time
- gradual retirement
- voluntary part-time work
- job sharing
- flexible work hours
- telework
- childcare solutions
- Employee Assistance Program (EAP)
- Special Leave policies.

Employees are also able to apply for extended leaves for personal and professional issues.

Toronto Auto Auctions

Address	8277 Lawson Road Milton, ON L9T 5C7
Telephone	1-800-667-4656
Fax	905-875-2910
Website	www.taacars.ca
Type of business	Car auction
Canadian locations	3
Total employees	1000
2005, 2006 Award categories	Recruitment Retention Workplace culture Management practices

The company

For the second consecutive year, Toronto Auto Auctions (TAA) of Milton, Ontario, is a recipient of a *Best Employers Award for 50 Plus Canadians™*. The company first applied on the urging of two of their employees who had seen a newspaper article about the awards. They suggested that TAA make a submission based on the large number of mature employees on the company's payroll. After all, they said, of the 800 people employed by Toronto Auto Auction, 500 are 50-plus! Ruth Hart, the company founder, continues to work as VP Business Development and is a role model for women in the traditionally male automotive world, continuing to lead well into her 70s.

History

Toronto Auto Auctions was the first weekly wholesale automotive auction in Canada. Detroit native Jack Hudelson opened Motor City Auto Auctions in west-end Toronto in 1952, which closed after 12 years of operation. In 1964, two of Motor City's original employees, Homer Stephens and Ruth Hart, reopened the auction with Stephens as auctioneer and Hart as office manager.

In 1983, TAA became the sixteenth auction purchased by Manheim Auctions, the world's leading provider of used vehicle services and marketplaces to professional buyers and sellers. Stephens and Hart were retained to manage the auction.

In 1986, Stephens passed away. Left to run the auction on her own, Hart and her dedicated staff, many of whom had been with the company since the early days, continued the auction's steady growth. In 1989, TAA moved to its present 64-acre site in Milton, Ontario.

Today, TAA is the largest vehicle auction in Canada, averaging sales of more than 4,500 cars weekly to registered motor vehicle dealers. Brad Hart (Ruth Hart and Homer Stephen's son) currently serves as General Manager while his mother has the position of Vice President, Canadian Business Development for Manheim.

Mature employees fit the bill

More than half of TAA's employees are 50-plus, and there is no mandatory retirement age (a policy in place long before it became mandatory in Ontario). Hiring so many older workers was not a deliberate business strategy, says Gary Fry, Operations Manager at TAA. Fry explains that auctions often take place at odd hours, for example, on a Tuesday morning from nine until one or on a Thursday evening from six to 10. "It just seems that the unpredictable hours of operation appeal more to retired people seeking additional income or the social interaction that comes from working."

TAA has found their older workers to be extremely adaptable and to bring a rich mosaic of skills, experience and knowledge to the organization. "Because of their life experience, their people skills are outstanding," says Fry. "They can easily step out of their role to offer personal assistance to other employees."

Toronto Auto Auctions has also found that a more mature workforce means lower turnover, low absenteeism and very low accident rates. Therefore, TAA makes every effort to retain its 50-plus employees by being flexible with work hours to allow people to spend time at their cottages in the summer or go south in the winter. In fact, more than 400 employees are part-time, a choice that works for all concerned.

Recruiting

Drivers and other employees at Toronto Auto Auctions come from all walks of life, from ex-firemen to ex-CEOs of companies.

In the past when Toronto Auto Auctions needed employees, they often hired young university students. But time and again that strategy backfired, as younger employees tended to damage property that didn't belong to TAA and damage the morale of the their more mature colleagues.

TAA's one regret is that there are not more women working in the automotive business. "They perceive the industry to be male-dominated and, as a result, we receive few applications from women," says Fry. "But female school bus drivers are perfect candidates for us. They can handle a large vehicle, multi-task and are quite prepared to deal with truancy!"

Health benefits

Toronto Auto Auctions accommodates employees who develop a physical ailment such as diabetes with flexible working arrangements (such as allowing them to take time out from their responsibilities to administer their insulin) and/or allowing them to switch to part-time work.

Benefits are generous and extend to those of the more than 400 part-time employees who work more than 30 hours per week. Benefits include eyeglasses, orthotics, physiotherapy and chiro-practic services, and private hospital room.

Advancement

There are promotions available to interested individuals, but TAA finds that many of its 50-plus employees are satisfied with part-time work and are not interested in having the responsibilities of full-time employment.

Retention

Since winning its first *Best Employers Award for 50 Plus Canadians*™ in 2006, Toronto Auto Auctions has established several committees to address issues raised in employee surveys and to further enhance the work experience for its predominantly 50-plus workforce. Their responsibilities are:

- production of a quarterly employee newsletter
- quarterly staff luncheons at which the GM presents a report to employees about the business
- employee orientation, now a formal process during which new hires learn about all departments at TAA, not just the one in which they will be working
- attire—this committee established an appropriate dress code and negotiates employee discounts for work boots and inclement weather clothing
- career opportunities are now formally posted to ensure equal opportunity and encourage promotions from within

- safety—while workplace safety has always been a company policy, more stringent efforts have been made to discourage employees from driving unsafe vehicles around the facility.

Statistics Canada

Address	100 Tunney's Pasture Driveway Ottawa, ON K1A 0T6
Telephone	613-951-1049
Fax	613-951-6181
Website	www.statcan.ca
Type of business	Government
Canadian locations	4
Total employees	4629
2007 Award categories	Management practices Career development

The organization

Statistics Canada's story is an incredible journey of continuing to refine their management practices over many years to ensure that employees are constantly challenged with new experiences and ready to respond to the government of the day's requests for data and information. Senior management vowed after downsizing a number of years back that they would not decimate their staff again. Statistics Canada developed an incredible flexibility in its practices to ensure that even in years when the budget is challenged, the organization would have the ability to move people around rather than let valued staff go.

The nature of work at Statistics Canada requires employees who possess high levels of skill and versatility. The demand for statistics changes rapidly due to changes in government budgets that affect those purchasing statistical data and services. Thus it is crucial for Statistics Canada to have a flexible workforce with transferable knowledge, skills and experience that can be redeployed when program priorities change. By encouraging long-term career employment, the agency is able to reap the rewards of its investment in training and development and optimize its employees' acquired skills.

Human Resources Management Strategy

Over the last 25 years, Statistics Canada has implemented a number of innovative policies, practices, and mechanisms that have evolved into a holistic Human Resources Management Strategy. This strategy engenders long-term career employment and enables Statistics Canada to leverage the talents of mature workers. Statistics Canada's Comprehensive Human Resources Management Strategy is based on four pillars that cover all aspects of human resources:

- hiring the best and the brightest
- investing in training and promoting a culture of continuous learning
- developing long-term career potential through career broadening assignments
- creating a positive work environment that encourages employee retention.

At Statistics Canada, human resources management is driven by a network of committees made up of executive-level managers. Each committee leads a major human resources program, such as recruitment, learning, internal staffing, career management, awards, wellness, and so on. The Human Resources Development Sub-committee oversees the work of these committees, guiding and assessing proposals and initiatives, and determining which should proceed for review and approval by the uppermost committee, the Human Resources Development Committee. This uppermost committee is the decision-making body that provides strategic direction on emerging HR issues and guidance to the HR management committees.

Human resources management is accepted as a primary responsibility for line managers at Statistics Canada and the majority of executive line managers are involved in at least one HR committee.

Recruitment and development

At Statistics Canada, there is a great deal of investment made in each employee, so entry-level professionals are chosen carefully.

Newly hired graduates are not placed immediately into a regular position. Instead, they are placed in a corporate pool for two years. During this period, they participate in an apprenticeship program that provides broad exposure to the agency. New recruits rotate among three or four assignments in various program divisions and participate in compulsory courses. Recruits are assigned mentors to help guide them for the duration of their program. Mentors are seasoned senior managers who have received training in mentoring. They have a broad knowledge of the skills required and their role is to help the recruit gain an overall perspective on the organization. The mentor also helps the recruit select assignments and training, and guides and supports the recruit's integration into the organizational culture.

Statistics Canada and 50-plus workers

An Alumni Program is in place that allows managers to hire retirees with specialized skills and expertise, such as corporate knowledge, analytical skills, subject matter and operational expertise.

Statistics Canada also has long-term career employees share their skills and expertise. The agency's succession planning is based on demographic analysis and forecasting, with strategic recruitment to fill pools. In recent years more than 50% of senior executives have retired and been replaced from internal succession pools. These succession pools are robust enough to withstand future retirements thanks to the knowledge transfer and expertise exchange made possible through career employees.

Continuous learning

More than 3% of the agency's salary budget is invested in training, resulting in an average of six days of formal training annually per employee.

The agency provides a full range of professional, technical, computer, management and human relations training opportunities at its on-campus Training Institute. Statistics Canada has some 30 full-time trainers, and a further 200 "guest lecturers"— employees or retired employees donating their time to training functions.

Continuous learning activities that span an employee's career are offered to employees and supplied in-house. Beyond the entry level, the organization provides a full range of optional professional and technical courses. In addition, Statistics Canada provides management training tailored to each managerial level. All new supervisors, middle managers and senior managers are required to take a number of formal courses and seminars, as well as participate in corporate task forces or working groups that address a corporate issue. This process provides exposure to senior management's decision-making process.

Statistics Canada has a formal Learning Policy that requires the establishment of divisional learning plans and encourages each employee to develop an individual learning plan. The annual performance review is used as an opportunity to encourage each employee to create a learning plan. At this point, each employee discusses training needs with his or her supervisor, both for the current job and for planned career moves within the agency. Employees are also offered a biennial "skip-level interview" with the supervisor's supervisor to discuss longer range training in order to meet career goals.

Workplace wellness

Ensuring that all employees feel valued helps encourage commitment, increase retention and facilitate mobility and versatility. A positive work environment helps achieve this goal. The Statistics Canada's Workplace Wellness Strategy focuses on five key areas:

1. Open communication

Some mechanisms in place to ensure two-way communication are: the annual "State of the Union Address" by the Chief Statistician; regular employee opinion surveys; and regular debriefings to all senior managers and their staff regarding the weekly Executive Committee meetings.

2. Valuing people

Key to Statistics Canada's commitment to employees is the no-lay-off policy stating that should it become necessary to reduce or eliminate a program due to budget reductions or changes in priority, affected employees will be moved to other areas requiring staff and will have absolute preference in staffing. Other initiatives include a network of senior Harassment Prevention Officers, an Employee Assistance Program, and an Informal Conflict Resolution Program.

3. Investment in employee facilities

The agency offers a number of onsite services that support active living, including a fitness and cardio facility, nursing services, and a day-care centre. The agency also has two Automated External Defibrillators (AEDs) onsite and a team of six employees trained in their use.

4. Providing employee activities

A few examples of employee activities are: the annual influenza immunization clinic; an annual Employee Appreciation Day; and lunch information sessions with speakers on topics such as nutrition, exercise, and stress management. There is also agency support for more than 100 employee clubs, organizations and committees.

5. Enabling a positive work-life balance

In addition to the normal leave provisions for vacation, sickness and family responsibilities, Statistics Canada offers a flexible work environment with options such as flex time, part-time, job sharing, compressed time and working from home.

Awards and Recognition

A formal Awards and Recognition Program consists of Instant Awards that can be given anytime to acknowledge specific contributions, and more formal awards presented annually, such as those for long service, individual and group merit awards, employee of the year, and a Career Excellence Award for retired employees in recognition of an outstanding career at Statistics Canada.

CHAPTER 8

Revolutionizing Your Workforce

KAA-BOOM! How to Engage the 50-Plus Workforce and Beat the Skills Shortage Crisis examines the various workforce trends that are expected to lead to talent shortages of unprecedented proportions. It introduces the *Workplace Institute Engagement Model for 50 Plus Workers™* and the elements organizations must consider to successfully engage the 50-plus workforce. It explores how redirecting the focus of current attraction and retention programs to include mature workers can help alleviate this coming crisis. Case studies of the strategies and practices of *Best Employers Award for 50 Plus Canadians™* winners demonstrate how elements of the engagement model can lead to organizational success.

This organizational reorientation towards 50-plus workers sounds elementary, but in practice it will require a revolution. Outdated, discriminatory attitudes towards 50-plus individuals need to be overturned and radically new policies, procedures and programs need to be championed. This revolution will have benefits far beyond attracting and retaining skilled mature workers and easing a chronic talent crunch. It will result in a productive, engaged and truly diverse workforce—one that contains people of all ages, all ethic groups and all cultural backgrounds.

KAA-BOOM! Start the revolution—and win

What does this workplace revolution require in order to succeed?

1. Leadership

In any organization, change begins at the top. Senior management must lead by example and champion fair and equitable hiring and retention policies for older workers. Senior managers need to be more attentive to workforce issues.

2. Management buy-in

Management must be committed to redirecting their hiring, training and retention policies and abandon stereotypes concerning older workers.

3. Supportive policies and programs

These need to be in place, ones that are fair and inclusive of all employees.

4. Training

Opportunities must not be restricted to younger workers.

5. Flexible work arrangements

6. Retirement planning programs

These are essential in retaining mature workers as well as helping them to leave, especially women who entered or re-entered the workforce later in life after raising families, or immigrants who started late in saving for retirement.

7. Family and eldercare supports

8. Targeted health and wellness initiatives

Organizations need to examine their particular demographic makeup and create health and wellness interventions that support the particular health risks and wellness needs of that demographic.

9. Creative roles for experienced workers

If you don't want them to leave—consider mentoring, special projects, advisory positions or a part-time option.

10. Downsized responsibilities

Many mature employees in key roles retire early due to demanding roles that require long hours. To retain these individuals, offer them the opportunity to reduce their workload or shift to less demanding roles on a voluntary basis while mentoring their successor or junior staff.

11. Leave and compensation options

While parental leaves are important to younger workers, sabbaticals and leaves of absence are attractive to older workers. A one-size-fits-all approach does not work for today's diverse workforce. Companies need to examine a "cafeteria-style" approach where employees can choose what programs and offerings most pertain to their needs at their particular stage in life.

12. Understanding workforce trends

Knowing the required skill sets your company will need in five, 10 or even 15 years (in cases of health professional requirements or scientific research) is essential. Lessening the impact of the coming talent shortage requires in-depth planning now.

Workforce planning: a checklist for your organization

Planning for the coming talent crunch begins today. Start by asking the following questions.

- Are your current staffing and skills requirements being met?
- Are you already having difficulty attracting and retaining certain skills?
- What are the business goals of the organization? Where is the business going to be in three years? Five years? Ten years?
- What skills will your organization need in three, five, and 10 years to meet those business goals? Will your required contingent of engineers, for example, increase over this time?
- What are your plans to fill those positions?
- What is the current demographic of your organization? If many of your essential workers are now 50-plus, how do you plan to retain or replace them?
- What are the future plans of your 50-plus staff? Conduct a survey and ask. Are they planning to retire early? Stay on? How many are in essential functions? How many possess vital industry knowledge? Who can you not do without? What it will take to induce them to stay?

Brave new world: the workforce of the future

For the last 50 years, human resources initiatives have centred on the attraction, development, and retention of the young. At a time when the under-30 demographic outnumbered their seniors, it made sense to concentrate training dollars on the development of younger employees who represented the future.

This hasn't changed. The young still represent the future and attracting, developing and retaining the best and brightest young people makes sense for the long-term business continuity of an organization. What has changed is that workforce demographics have reversed themselves and the 40-plus cohort now outnumbers the under-30s. There simply aren't enough talented, skilled younger individuals available to replace the millions of retiring baby boomers. This means a new reality for human resources and organizations throughout the western world.

The new reality is this: businesses need to attract, retain and develop workers of all ages.

The revolution has begun. There will be winners and losers. Those who refuse to acknowledge that change is in the air will not survive. The future belongs to the young, but it is the aging boomers who will take them there.

KAA-BOOM!

ISBN 142511624-8